The Science of Getting Rich

Wallace D. Wattles

The Master Key System

Charles Haanel

THE SCIENCE OF GETTING RICH

By

Wallace D. Wattles

TABLE OF CONTENTS

PREFACE

THIS book is pragmatical, not philosophical; a practical manual, not a treatise upon theories. It is intended for the men and women whose most pressing need is for money; who wish to get rich first, and philosophize afterward. It is for those who have, so far, found neither the time, the means, nor the opportunity to go deeply into the study of metaphysics, but who want results and who are willing to take the conclusions of science as a basis for action, without going into all the processes by which those conclusions were reached.

It is expected that the reader will take the fundamental statements upon faith, just as he would take statements concerning a law of electrical action if they were promulgated by a Marconi or an Edison; and, taking the statements upon faith, that he will prove their truth by acting upon them without fear or hesitation. Every man or woman who does this will certainly get rich; for the science herein applied is an exact science, and failure is impossible. For the benefit, however, of those who wish to investigate philosophical theories and so secure a logical basis for faith, I will here cite certain authorities.

The monistic theory of the universe the theory that One is All, and that All is One; That one Substance manifests itself as the seeming many elements of the material world -is of Hindu origin, and has been gradually winning its way into the thought of the western world for two hundred years. It is the foundation of all the Oriental philosophies, and of those of Descartes, Spinoza, Leibnitz, Schopenhauer, Hegel, and Emerson. The reader who would dig to the philosophical foundations of this is advised to read Hegel and Emerson for himself.

In writing this book I have sacrificed all other considerations to plainness and simplicity of style, so that all might understand. The plan of action laid down therein was deduced from the conclusions of philosophy; it has been thoroughly tested, and bears the supreme test of practical experiment; it works. If you wish to know how the conclusions were arrived at, read the writings of the authors mentioned above; and if you wish to reap the fruits of their philosophies in actual practice, read this book and do exactly as it tells you to do.

Wallace D. Wattles

CHAPTER 1 :The Right To Be Rich

WHATEVER may be said in praise of poverty, the fact remains that it is not possible to live a really complete or successful life unless one is rich. No man can rise to his greatest possible height in talent or soul development unless he has plenty of money; for to unfold the soul and to develop talent he must have many things to use, and he cannot have these things unless he has money to buy them with.

A man develops in mind, soul, and body by making use of things, and society is so organized that man must have money in order to become the possessor of things; therefore, the basis of all advancement for man must be the science of getting rich.

The object of all life is development; and everything that lives has an inalienable right to all the development it is capable of attaining. Man's right to life means his right to have the free and unrestricted use of all the things which may be necessary to his fullest mental, spiritual, and physical unfoldment; or, in other words, his right to be rich.

In this book, I shall not speak of riches in a figurative way; to be really rich does not mean to be satisfied or contented with a little. No man ought to be satisfied with a little if he is capable of using and enjoying more. The purpose of Nature is the advancement and unfoldment of life; and every man should have all that can contribute to the power; elegance, beauty, and richness of life; to be content with less is sinful.

The man who owns all he wants for the living of all the life he is capable of living is rich; and no man who has not plenty of money can have all he wants. Life has advanced so far, and become so complex, that even the most ordinary man or woman requires a great amount of wealth in order to live in a manner that even approaches completeness. Every person naturally wants to become all that they are capable of becoming; this desire to realize innate possibilities is inherent in human nature; we cannot help wanting to be all that we can be. Success in life is becoming what you want to be; you can become what you want to be only by making use of things, and you can have the free use of things only as you become rich enough to buy them. To understand the science of getting rich is therefore the most essential of all knowledge.

There is nothing wrong in wanting to get rich. The desire for riches is really the desire for a richer, fuller, and more abundant life; and that desire is praise worthy. The man who does not desire to live more abundantly is abnormal, and so the man who does not desire to have money enough to by all he wants is abnormal.

There are three motives for which we live; we live for the body, we live for the mind, we live for the soul. No one of these is better or holier than the other; all are alike desirable, and no one of the three--body, mind, or soul--can live fully if either of the others is cut short of full life and expression. It is not right or noble to live only for the soul and deny mind or body; and it is wrong to live for the intellect and deny body or soul.

We are all acquainted with the loathsome consequences of living for the body and denying both mind and soul; and we see that real life means the complete expression of all that man can give forth through body, mind, and soul. Whatever he can say, no man can be really happy or satisfied unless his body is living fully in every function, and unless the same is true of his mind and his soul. Wherever there is unexpressed possibility, or function not performed, there is unsatisfied desire. Desire is possibility seeking expression, or function seeking performance.

Man cannot live fully in body without good food, comfortable clothing, and warm shelter; and without freedom from excessive toil. Rest and recreation are also necessary to his physical life. He cannot live fully in mind without books and time to study them, without opportunity for travel and observation, or without intellectual companionship. To live fully in mind he must have intellectual recreations, and must surround himself with all the objects of art and beauty he is capable of using and appreciating. To live fully in soul, man must have love; and love is denied expression by poverty.

A man's highest happiness is found in the bestowal of benefits on those he loves; love finds its most natural and spontaneous expression in giving. The man who has nothing to give cannot fill his place as a husband or father, as a citizen, or as a man. It is in the use of material things that a man finds full life for his body, develops his mind, and unfolds his soul. It is therefore of supreme importance to him that he should be rich.

It is perfectly right that you should desire to be rich; if you are a normal man or woman you cannot help doing so. It is perfectly right that you should give your best attention to the Science of Getting Rich, for it is the noblest and most

11

necessary of all studies. If you neglect this study, you are derelict in your duty to yourself, to God and humanity; for you can render to God and humanity no greater service than to make the most of yourself.

CHAPTER 2: There is A Science of Getting Rich

THERE is a Science of getting rich, and it is an exact science, like algebra or arithmetic. There are certain laws which govern the process of acquiring riches; once these laws are learned and obeyed by any man, he will get rich with mathematical certainty.

The ownership of money and property comes as a result of doing things in a certain way; those who do things in this Certain Way, whether on purpose or accidentally, get rich; while those who do not do things in this Certain Way, no matter how hard they work or how able they are, remain poor. It is a natural law that like causes always produce like effects; and, therefore, any man or woman who learns to do things in this certain way will infallibly get rich.

That the above statement is true is shown by the following facts:

Getting rich is not a matter of environment, for, if it were, all the people in certain neighborhoods would become wealthy; the people of one city would all be rich, while those of other towns would all be poor; or the inhabitants of one state would roll in wealth, while those of an adjoining state would be in poverty.

But everywhere we see rich and poor living side by side, in the same environment, and often engaged in the same vocations. When two men are in the same locality, and in the same business, and one gets rich while the other remains poor, it shows that getting rich is not, primarily, a matter of environment. Some environments may be more favorable than others, but when two men in the same business are in the same neighborhood, and one gets rich while the other fails, it indicates that getting rich is the result of doing things in a Certain Way.

And further, the ability to do things in this certain way is not due solely to the possession of talent, for many people who have great talent remain poor, while other who have very little talent get rich. Studying the people who have got rich, we find that they are an average lot in all respects, having no greater talents and abilities than other men. It is evident that they do not get rich because they possess talents and abilities that other men have not, but because they happen to do things in a Certain Way. Getting rich is not the result of saving, or "thrift"; many very penurious people are poor, while free spenders often get rich. Nor is getting rich due to doing things which others fail to do; for two men in the same business often do almost exactly the same things, and one gets rich while the other remains poor or becomes bankrupt.

From all these things, we must come to the conclusion that getting rich is the result of doing things in a Certain Way. If getting rich is the result of doing things in a Certain Way, and if like causes always produce like effects, then any man or woman who can do things in that way can become rich, and the whole matter is brought within the domain of exact science.

The question arises here, whether this Certain Way may not be so difficult that only a few may follow it. This cannot be true, as we have seen, so far as natural ability is concerned. Talented people get rich, and blockheads get rich; intellectually brilliant people get rich, and very stupid people get rich; physically strong people get rich, and weak and sickly people get rich. Some degree of ability to think and understand is, of course, essential; but in so far natural ability is concerned, any man or woman who has sense enough to read and understand these words can certainly get rich. Also, we have seen that it is not a matter of environment. Location counts for something; one would not go to the heart of the Sahara and expect to do successful business.

Getting rich involves the necessity of dealing with men, and of being where there are people to deal with; and if these people are inclined to deal in the way you want to deal, so much the better. But that is about as far as environment goes.

If anybody else in your town can get rich, so can you; and if anybody else in your state can get rich, so can you. Again, it is not a matter of choosing some particular business or profession. People get rich in every business, and in every profession; while their next door neighbors in the same vocation remain in poverty. It is true that you will do best in a business which you like, and which is congenial to you; and if you have certain talents which are well developed, you will do best in a business which calls for the exercise of those talents. Also, you will do best in a business which is suited to your locality; an icecream parlor would do better in a warm climate than in Greenland, and a salmon fishery will succeed better in the Northwest than in Florida, where there are no salmon.

But, aside from these general limitations, getting rich is not dependent upon your engaging in some particular business, but upon your learning to do things

14

in a Certain Way. If you are now in business, and anybody else in your locality is getting rich in the same business, while you are not getting rich, it is because you are not doing things in the same Way that the other person is doing them. No one is prevented from getting rich by lack of capital. True, as you get capital the increase becomes more easy and rapid; but one who has capital is already rich, and does not need to consider how to become so.

No matter how poor you may be, if you begin to do things in the Certain Way you will begin to get rich; and you will begin to have capital. The getting of capital is a part of the process of getting rich; and it is a part of the result which invariably follows the doing of things in the Certain Way. You may be the poorest man on the continent, and be deeply in debt; you may have neither friends, influence, nor resources; but if you begin to do things in this way, you must infallibly begin to get rich, for like causes must produce like effects. If you have no capital, you can get capital; if you are in the wrong business, you can get into the right business; if you are in the wrong location, you can go to the right location; and you can do so by beginning in your present business and in your present location to do things in the Certain Way which causes success.

CHAPTER 3 : Is Opportunity Monopolized?

NO man is kept poor because opportunity has been taken away from him; because other people have monopolized the wealth, and have put a fence around it. You may be shut off from engaging in business in certain lines, but there are other channels open to you. Probably it would be hard for you to get control of any of the great railroad systems; that field is pretty well monopolized. But the electric railway business is still in its infancy, and offers plenty of scope for enterprise; and it will be but a very few years until traffic and transportation through the air will become a great industry, and in all its branches will give employment to hundreds of thousands, and perhaps to millions, of people. Why not turn your attention to the development of aerial transportation, instead of competing with J.J. Hill and others for a chance in the steam railway world?

It is quite true that if you are a workman in the employ of the steel trust you have very little chance of becoming the owner of the plant in which you work; but it is also true that if you will commence to act in a Certain Way, you can soon leave the employ of the steel trust; you can buy a farm of from ten to forty acres, and engage in business as a producer of foodstuffs. There is great opportunity at this time for men who will live upon small tracts of land and cultivate the same intensively; such men will certainly get rich. You may say that it is impossible for you to get the land, but I am going to prove to you that it is not impossible, and that you can certainly get a farm if you will go to work in a Certain Way.

At different periods the tide of opportunity sets in different directions, according to the needs of the whole, and the particular stage of social evolution which has been reached. At present, in America, it is setting toward agriculture and the allied industries and professions. Today, opportunity is open before the factory worker in his line. It is open before the business man who supplies the farmer more than before the one who supplies the factory worker; and before the professional man who waits upon the farmer more than before the one who serves the working class. There is abundance of opportunity for the man who will go with the tide, instead of trying to swim against it.

So the factory workers, either as individuals or as a class, are not deprived of opportunity. The workers are not being "kept down" by their masters; they are not being "ground" by the trusts and combinations of capital. As a class, they are where they are because they do not do things in a Certain Way. If the workers of America chose to do so, they could follow the example of their brothers in Belgium and other countries, and establish great department stores and co-operative industries; they could elect men of their own class to office, and pass laws favoring the development of such co-operative industries; and in a few years they could take peaceable possession of the industrial field.

The working class may become the master class whenever they will begin to do things in a Certain Way; the law of wealth is the same for them as it is for all others. This they must learn; and they will remain where they are as long as they continue to do as they do. The individual worker, however, is not held down by the ignorance or the mental slothfulness of his class; he can follow the tide of opportunity to riches, and this book will tell him how.

No one is kept in poverty by a shortness in the supply of riches; there is more than enough for all. A palace as large as the capitol at Washington might be built for every family on earth from the building material in the United States alone; and under intensive cultivation, this country would produce wool, cotton, linen, and silk enough to cloth each person in the world finer than Solomon was arrayed in all his glory; together with food enough to feed them all luxuriously.

The visible supply is practically inexhaustible; and the invisible supply really IS inexhaustible. Everything you see on earth is made from one original substance, out of which all things proceed. New Forms are constantly being made, and older ones are dissolving; but all are shapes assumed by One Thing. There is no limit to the supply of Formless Stuff, or Original Substance. The universe is made out of it; but it was not all used in making the universe. The spaces in, through, and between the forms of the visible universe are permeated and filled with the Original Substance; with the formless Stuff; with the raw material of all things. Ten thousand times as much as has been made might still be made, and even then we should not have exhausted the supply of universal raw material.

No man, therefore, is poor because nature is poor, or because there is not enough to go around. Nature is an inexhaustible storehouse of riches; the supply will never run short. Original Substance is alive with creative energy, and is constantly producingmore forms. When the supply of building material is exhausted, more will be produced; when the soil is exhausted so that food stuffs and materials for Clothing will no longer grow upon it, it will be renewed or more soil will be made. When all the gold and silver has been dug from the earth, if man is still in such a stage of social development that he needs gold and silver, more will produced from the Formless. The Formless Stuff responds to the needs of man; it will not let him be without any good thing.

This is true of man collectively; the race as a whole is always abundantly rich, and if individuals are poor, it is because they do not follow the Certain Way of doing things which makes the individual man rich. The Formless Stuff is intelligent; it is stuff which thinks. It is alive, and is always impelled toward more life.

It is the natural and inherent impulse of life to seek to live more; it is the nature of intelligence to enlarge itself, and of consciousness to seek to extend its boundaries and find fuller expression. The universe of forms has been made by Formless Living Substance, throwing itself into form in order to express itself more fully. The universe is a great Living Presence, always moving inherently toward more life and fuller functioning. Nature is formed for the advancement of life; its impelling motive is the increase of life. For this cause, everything which can possibly minister to life is bountifully provided; there can be no lack unless God is to contradict himself and nullify his own works.

You are not kept poor by lack in the supply of riches; it is a fact which I shall demonstrate a little farther on that even the resources of the Formless Supply are at the command of the man or woman will act and think in a Certain Way.

CHAPTER 4 : The First Principle in The Science of Getting Rich

THOUGHT is the only power which can produce tangible riches from the Formless Substance. The stuff from which all things are made is a substance which thinks, and a thought of form in this substance produces the form. Original Substance moves according to its thoughts; every form and process you see in nature is the visible expression of a thought in Original Substance. As the Formless Stuff thinks of a form, it takes that form; as it thinks of a motion, it makes that motion. That is the way all things were created. We live in a thought world, which is part of a thought universe. The thought of a moving universe extended throughout Formless Substance, and the Thinking Stuff moving according to that thought, took the form of systems of planets, and maintains that form. Thinking Substance takes the form of its thought, and moves according to the thought.

Holding the idea of a circling system of suns and worlds, it takes the form of these bodies, and moves them as it thinks. Thinking the form of a slow-growing oak tree, it moves accordingly, and produces the tree, though centuries may be required to do the work. In creating, the Formless seems to move according to the lines of motion it has established; the thought of an oak tree does not cause the instant formation of a full-grown tree, but it does start in motion the forces which will produce the tree, along established lines of growth. Every thought of form, held in thinking Substance, causes the creation of the form, but always, or at least generally, along lines of growth and action already established.

The thought of a house of a certain construction, if it were impressed upon Formless Substance, might not cause the instant formation, of the house; but it would cause the turning of creative energies already working in trade and commerce into such channels as to result in the speedy building of the house. And if there were no existing channels through which the creative energy could work, then the house would be formed directly from primal substance, without waiting for the slow processes of the organic and inorganic world. No thought of form can be impressed upon Original Substance without causing the creation of the form.

Man is a thinking center, and can originate thought. All the forms that man fashions with his hands must first exist in his thought; he cannot shape a thing until he has thought that thing. And so far man has confined his efforts wholly

19

to the work of his hands; he has applied manual labor to the world of forms, seeking to change or modify those already existing. He has never thought of trying to cause the creation of new forms by impressing his thoughts upon Formless Substance. When man has a thought-form, he takes material from the forms of nature, and makes an image of the form which is in his mind. He has, so far, made little or no effort to co-operate with Formless Intelligence; to work "with the Father." He has not dreamed that he can "do what he seeth the Father doing." Man reshapes and modifies existing forms by manual labor; he has given no attention to the question whether he may not produce things from Formless Substance by communicating his thoughts to it. We propose to prove that he may do so; to prove that any man or woman may do so, and to show how.

As our first step, we must lay down three fundamental propositions.

First, we assert that there is one original formless stuff, or substance, from which all things are made. All the seemingly many elements are but different presentations of one element; all the many forms found in organic and inorganic nature are but different shapes, made from the same stuff. And this stuff is thinking stuff; a thought held in it produces the form of the thought. Thought, in thinking substance, produces shapes. Man is a thinking center, capable of original thought; if man can communicate his thought to original thinking substance, he can cause the creation, or formation, of the thing he thinks about.

To summarize this:

There is a thinking stuff from which all things are made, and which, in its original state, permeates, penetrates, and fills the interspaces of the universe. A thought, in this substance, produces the thing that is imaged by the thought. Man can form things in his thought, and, by impressing his thought upon formless substance, can cause the thing he thinks about to be created.

It may be asked if I can prove these statements; and without going into details, I answer that I can do so, both by logic and experience. Reasoning back from the phenomena of form and thought, I come to one original thinking substance; and reasoning forward from this thinking substance, I come to man's power to cause the formation of the thing he thinks about.

And by experiment, I find the reasoning true; and this is my strongest proof. If one man who reads this book gets rich by doing what it tells him to do, that is evidence in support of my claim; but if every man who does what it tells him to do gets rich, that is positive proof until some one goes through the process and fails. The theory is true until the process fails; and this process will not fail, for every man who does exactly what this book tells him to do will get rich.

I have said that men get rich by doing things in a Certain Way; and in order to do so, men must become able to think in a certain way. A man's way of doing things is the direct result of the way he thinks about things. To do things in a way you want to do them, you will have to acquire the ability to think the way you want to think; this is the first step toward getting rich. To think what you want to think is to think TRUTH, regardless of appearances. Every man has the natural and inherent power to think what he wants to think, but it requires far more effort to do so than it does to think the thoughts which are suggested by appearances. To think according to appearance is easy; to think truth regardless of appearances is laborious, and requires the expenditure of more power than any other workman is called upon to perform.

There is no labor from which most people shrink as they do from that of sustained and consecutive thought; it is the hardest work in the world. This is especially true when truth is contrary to appearances. Every appearance in the visible world tends to produce a corresponding form in the mind which observes it; and this can only be prevented by holding the thought of the TRUTH.

To look upon the appearance of disease will produce the form of disease in your own mind, and ultimately in your body, unless you hold the thought of the truth, which is that there is no disease; it is only an appearance, and the reality is health. To look upon the appearances of poverty will produce corresponding forms in your own mind, unless you hold to the truth that there is no poverty; there is only abundance. To think health when surrounded by the appearances of disease, or to think riches when in the midst of appearances of poverty, requires power; but he who acquires this power becomes a MASTER MIND. He can conquer fate; he can have what he wants.

This power can only be acquired by getting hold of the basic fact which is behind all appearances; and that fact is that there is one Thinking Substance, from which and by which all things are made. Then we must grasp the truth that every thought held in this substance becomes a form, and that man can so impress his thoughts upon it as to cause them to take form and become visible things.

When we realize this, we lose all doubt and fear, for we know that we can create what we want to create; we can get what we want to have, and can become what we want to be. As a first step toward getting rich, you must believe the three fundamental statements given previously in this chapter; and in order to emphasize them. I repeat them here:

There is a thinking stuff from which all things are made, and which, in its original state, permeates, penetrates, and fills the interspaces of the universe. A thought, in this substance, Produces the thing that is imaged by the thought. Man can form things in his thought, and, by impressing his thought upon formless substance, can cause the thing he thinks about to be created. You must lay aside all other concepts of the universe than this monistic one; and you must dwell upon this until it is fixed in your mind, and has become your habitual thought.

Read these creed statements over and over again; fix every word upon your memory, and meditate upon them until you firmly believe what they say. If a doubt comes to you, cast it aside as a sin. Do not listen to arguments against this idea; do not go to churches or lectures where a contrary concept of things is taught or preached. Do not read magazines or books which teach a different idea; if you get mixed up in your faith, all your efforts will be in vain. Do not ask why these things are true, nor speculate as to how they can be true; simply take them on trust. The science of getting rich begins with the absolute acceptance of this faith.

CHAPTER 5 : Increasing Life

YOU must get rid of the last vestige of the old idea that there is a Deity whose will it is that you should be poor, or whose purposes may be served by keeping you in poverty. The Intelligent Substance which is All, and in All, and which lives in All and

lives in you, is a consciously Living Substance. Being a consciously living substance, It must have the nature and inherent desire of every living intelligence for increase of life. Every living thing must continually seek for the enlargement of its life, because life, in the mere act of living, must increase itself.

A seed, dropped into the ground, springs into activity, and in the act of living produces a hundred more seeds; life, by living, multiplies itself. It is forever becoming More; it must do so, if it continues to be at all. Intelligence is under this same necessity for continuous increase. Every thought we think makes it necessary for us to think another thought; consciousness is continually expanding. Every fact we learn leads us to the learning of another fact; knowledge is continually increasing. Every talent we cultivate brings to the mind the desire to cultivate another talent; we are subject to the urge of life, seeking expression, which ever drives us on to know more, to do more, and to be more.

In order to know more, do more, and be more we must have more; we must have things to use, for we learn, and do, and become, only by using things. We must get rich, so that we can live more.

The desire for riches is simply the capacity for larger life seeking fulfillment; every desire is the effort of an unexpressed possibility to come into action. It is power seeking to manifest which causes desire. That which makes you want more money is the same as that which makes the plant grow; it is Life, seeking fuller expression.

The One Living Substance must be subject to this inherent law of all life; it is permeated with the desire to live more; that is why it is under the necessity of creating things. The One Substance desires to live more in you; hence it wants you to have all the things you can use. It is the desire of God that you should get rich. He wants you to get rich because he can express himself better through you if you have plenty of things to use in giving him expression. He can live more in you if you have unlimited command of the means of life.

The universe desires you to have everything you want to have. Nature is friendly to your plans. Everything is naturally for you. Make up your mind that this is true. It is essential, however that your purpose should harmonize with the purpose that is in All. You must want real life, not mere pleasure of sensual gratification. Life is the performance of function; and the individual really lives only when he performs every function, physical, mental, and spiritual, of which he is capable, without excess in any.

You do not want to get rich in order to live swinishly, for the gratification of animal desires; that is not life. But the performance of every physical function is a part of life, and no one lives completely who denies the impulses of the body a normal and healthful expression. You do not want to get rich solely to enjoy mental pleasures, to get knowledge, to gratify ambition, to outshine others, to be famous. All these are a legitimate part of life, but the man who lives for the pleasures of the intellect alone will only have a partial life, and he will never be satisfied with his lot. You do not want to get rich solely for the good of others, to lose yourself for the salvation of mankind, to experience the joys of philanthropy and sacrifice. The joys of the soul are only a part of life; and they are no better or nobler than any other part.

You want to get rich in order that you may eat, drink, and be merry when it is time to do these things; in order that you may surround yourself with beautiful things, see distant lands, feed your mind, and develop your intellect; in order that you may love men and do kind things, and be able to play a good part in helping the world to find truth.

But remember that extreme altruism is no better and no nobler than extreme selfishness; both are mistakes. Get rid of the idea that God wants you to sacrifice yourself for others, and that you can secure his favor by doing so; God requires nothing of the kind. What he wants is that you should make the most of yourself, for yourself, and for others; and you can help others more by making the most of yourself than in any other way. You can make the most of yourself only by getting rich; so it is right and praiseworthy that you should give your first and best thought to the work of acquiring wealth.

Remember, however, that the desire of Substance is for all, and its movements must be for more life to all; it cannot be made to work for less life to any, because it is equally in all, seeking riches and life. Intelligent Substance will make things for you, but it will not take things away from some one else and give them to you. You must get rid of the thought of competition. You are to create, not to compete for what is already created. You do not have to take anything away from any one. You do not have to drive sharp bargains. You do not have to cheat, or to take advantage. You do not need to let any man work for you for less than he earns. You do not have to covet the property of others, or to look at it with wishful eyes; no man has anything of which you cannot have the like, and that without taking what he has away from him. You are to become a creator, not a competitor; you are going to get what you want, but in such a way that when you get it every other man will have more than he has now.

I am aware that there are men who get a vast amount of money by proceeding in direct opposition to the statements in the paragraph above, and may add a word of explanation here. Men of the plutocratic type, who become very rich, do so sometimes purely by their extraordinary ability on the plane of competition; and sometimes they unconsciously relate themselves to Substance in its great purposes and movements for the general racial upbuilding through industrial evolution. Rockefeller, Carnegie, Morgan, et al., have been the unconscious agents of the Supreme in the necessary work of systematizing and organizing productive industry; and in the end, their work will contribute immensely toward increased life for all.

Their day is nearly over; they have organized production, and will soon be succeeded by the agents of the multitude, who will organize the machinery of distribution. The multi-millionaires are like the monster reptiles of the prehistoric eras; they play a necessary part in the evolutionary process, but the same Power which produced them will dispose of them. And it is well to bear in mind that they have never been really rich; a record of the private lives of most of this class will show that they have really been the most abject and wretched of the poor. Riches secured on the competitive plane are never satisfactory and permanent; they are yours today, and another's tomorrow.

Remember, if you are to become rich in a scientific and certain way, you must rise entirely out of the competitive thought. You must never think for a moment that the supply is limited. Just as soon as you begin to think that all the money is being "cornered" and controlled by bankers and others, and that you must exert yourself to get laws passed to stop this process, and so on; in that moment you drop into the competitive mind, and your power to cause creation is gone for the time being; and what is worse, you will probably arrest the creative movements you have already instituted.

KNOW that there are countless millions of dollars' worth of gold in the mountains of the earth, not yet brought to light; and know that if there were not, more would be created from Thinking Substance to supply your needs. KNOW that the money you need will come, even if it is necessary for a thousand men to be led to the discovery of new gold mines to-morrow. Never look at the visible supply; look always at the limitless riches in Formless Substance, and KNOW that they are coming to you as fast as you can receive and use them. Nobody, by cornering the visible supply, can prevent you from getting what is yours.

So never allow yourself to think for an instant that all the best building spots will be taken before you get ready to build your house, unless you hurry. Never worry about the trusts and combines, and get anxious for fear they will soon come to own the whole earth. Never get afraid that you will lose what you want because some other person "beats you to it." That cannot possibly happen; you are not seeking any thing that is possessed by anybody else; you are causing what you want to be created from formless Substance, and the supply is without limits.

Stick to the formulated statement:

There is a thinking stuff from which all things are made, and which, in its original state, permeates, penetrates, and fills the interspaces of the universe. A thought, in this substance, produces the thing that is imaged by the thought. Man can form things in his thought, and, by impressing his thought upon formless substance, can cause the thing he thinks about to be created.

CHAPTER 6 : How Riches Come to You

WHEN I say that you do not have to drive sharp bargains, I do not mean that you do not have to drive any bargains at all, or that you are above the necessity for having any dealings with your fellow men. I mean that you will not need to deal with them unfairly; you do not have to get something for nothing, but can give to every man more than you take from him.

You cannot give every man more in cash market value than you take from him, but you can give him more in use value than the cash value of the thing you take from him. The paper, ink, and other material in this book may not be worth the money you pay for it; but if the ideas suggested by it bring you thousands of dollars, you have not been wronged by those who sold it to you; they have given you a great use value for a small cash value.

Let us suppose that I own a picture by one of the great artists, which, in any civilized community, is worth thousands of dollars. I take it to Baffin Ray, and by "salesmanship" induce an Eskimo to give a bundle of furs worth $ 500 for it. I have really wronged him, for he has no use for the picture; it has no use value to him; it will not add to his life. But suppose I give him a gun worth $50 for his furs; then he has made a good bargain. He has use for the gun; it will get him many more furs and much food; it will add to his life in every way; it will make him rich.

When you rise from the competitive to the creative plane, you can scan your business transactions very strictly, and if you are selling any man anything which does not add more to his life than the thing he give you in exchange, you can afford to stop it. You do not have to beat anybody in business. And if you are in a business which does beat people, get out of it at once. Give every man more in use value than you take from him in cash value; then you are adding to the life of the world by every business transaction. If you have people working for you, you must take from them more in cash value than you pay them in wages; but you can so organize your business that it will be filled with the principle of advancement, and so that each employee who wishes to do so may advance a little every day. You can make your business do for your employees what this book is doing for you. You can so conduct your business that it will be a sort of ladder, by which every employee who will take the trouble may climb

27

to riches himself; and given the opportunity, if he will not do so it is not your fault.

And finally, because you are to cause the creation of your riches from Formless Substance which permeates all your environment, it does not follow that they are to take shape from the atmosphere and come into being before your eyes. If you want a sewing machine, for instance, I do not mean to tell you that you are to impress the thought of a sewing machine on Thinking Substance until the machine is formed without hands, in the room where you sit, or elsewhere. But if you want a sewing machine, hold the mental image of it with the most positive certainty that it is being made, or is on its way to you. After once forming the thought, have the most absolute and unquestioning faith that the sewing machine is coming; never think of it, or speak, of it, in any other way than as being sure to arrive. Claim it as already yours.

It will be brought to you by the power of the Supreme Intelligence, acting upon the minds of men. If you live in Maine, it may be that a man will be brought from Texas or Japan to engage in some transaction which will result in your getting what you want. If so, the whole matter will be as much to that man's advantage as it is to yours.

Do not forget for a moment that the Thinking Substance is through all, in all, communicating with all, and can influence all. The desire of Thinking Substance for fuller life and better living has caused the creation of all the sewing machines already made; and it can cause the creation of millions more, and will, whenever men set it in motion by desire and faith, and by acting in a Certain Way.

You can certainly have a sewing machine in your house; and it is just as certain that you can have any other thing or things which you want, and which you will use for the advancement of your own life and the lives of others.

You need not hesitate about asking largely. Original Substance wants to live all that is possible in you, and wants you to have all that you can or will use for the living of the most abundant life. If you fix upon your consciousness the fact that the desire you feel for the possession of riches is one with the desire of Omnipotence for more complete expression, your faith becomes invincible.

Once I saw a little boy sitting at a piano, and vainly trying to bring harmony out of the keys; and I saw that he was grieved and provoked by his inability to play real music. I asked him the cause of his vexation, and he answered, "I can feel the music in me, but I can't make my hands go right." The music in him was the

URGE of Original Substance, containing all the possibilities of all life; all that there is of music was seeking expression through the child.

God, the One Substance, is trying to live and do and enjoy things through humanity. He is saying "I want hands to build wonderful structures, to play divine harmonies, to paint glorious pictures; I want feet to run my errands, eyes to see my beauties, tongues to tell mighty truths and to sing marvelous songs," and so on. All that there is of possibility is seeking expression through men. God wants those who can play music to have pianos and every other instrument, and to have the means to cultivate their talents to the fullest extent; He wants those who can appreciate beauty to be able to surround themselves with beautiful things; He wants those who can discern truth to have every opportunity to travel and observe; He wants those who can appreciate dress to be beautifully clothed, and those who can appreciate good food to be luxuriously fed. He wants all these things because it is Himself that enjoys and appreciates them; it is God who wants to play, and sing, and enjoy beauty, and proclaim truth and wear fine clothes, and eat good foods. "It is God that worketh in you to will and to do," said Paul.

The desire you feel for riches is the infinite, seeking to express Himself in you as He sought to find expression in the little boy at the piano. So you need not hesitate to ask largely. Your part is to focalize and express the desire to God.

This is a difficult point with most people; they retain something of the old idea that poverty and self-sacrifice are pleasing to God. They look upon poverty as a part of the plan, a necessity of nature. They have the idea that God has finished His work, and made all that He can make, and that the majority of men must stay poor because there is not enough to go around. They hold to so much of this erroneous thought that they feel ashamed to ask for wealth; they try not to want more than a very modest competence, just enough to make them fairly comfortable.

I recall now the case of one student who was told that he must get in mind a clear picture of the things he desired, so that the creative thought of them might be impressed on Formless Substance. He was a very poor man, living in a rented house, and having only what he earned from day to day; and he could not grasp the fact that all wealth was his. So, after thinking the matter over, he decided that he might reasonably ask for a new rug for the floor of his best room, and an anthracite coal stove to heat the house during the cold weather. Following the instructions given in this book, he obtained these things in a few months; and then it dawned upon him that he had not asked enough. He went

29

through the house in which he lived, and planned all the improvements he would like to make in it; he mentally added a bay window here and a room there, until it was complete in his mind as his ideal home; and then he planned its furnishings.

Holding the whole picture in his mind, he began living in the Certain Way, and moving toward what he wanted; and he owns the house now, and is rebuilding it after the form of his mental image. And now, with still larger faith, he is going on to get greater things. It has been unto him according to his faith, and it is so with you and with all of us.

CHAPTER 7 : Gratitude

THE illustrations given in the last chapter will have conveyed to the reader the fact that the first step toward getting rich is to convey the idea of your wants to the Formless Substance. This is true, and you will see that in order to do so it becomes necessary to relate yourself to the Formless Intelligence in a harmonious way. To secure this harmonious relation is a matter of such primary and vital importance that I shall give some space to its discussion here, and give you instructions which, if you will follow them, will be certain to bring you into perfect unity of mind with God.

The whole process of mental adjustment and atonement can be summed up in one word, gratitude.

First, you believe that there is one Intelligent Substance, from which all things proceed; second, you believe that this Substance gives you everything you desire; and third, you relate yourself to it by a feeling of deep and profound gratitude.

Many people who order their lives rightly in all other ways are kept in poverty by their lack of gratitude. Having received one gift from God, they cut the wires which connect them with Him by failing to make acknowledgment. It is easy to understand that the nearer we live to the source of wealth, the more wealth we shall receive; and it is easy also to understand that the soul that is always grateful lives in closer touch with God than the one which never looks to Him in thankful acknowledgment.

The more gratefully we fix our minds on the Supreme when good things come to us, the more good things we will receive, and the more rapidly they will come; and the reason simply is that the mental attitude of gratitude draws the mind into closer touch with the source from which the blessings come. If it is a new thought to you that gratitude brings your whole mind into closer harmony with the creative energies of the universe, consider it well, and you will see that it is true. The good things you already have have come to you along the line of obedience to certain laws. Gratitude will lead your mind out along the ways by which things come; and it will keep you in close harmony with creative thought and prevent you from falling into competitive thought. Gratitude alone can keep you looking toward the All, and prevent you from falling into the error of thinking of the supply as limited; and to do that would be fatal to your hopes.

There is a Law of Gratitude, and it is absolutely necessary that you should observe the law, if you are to get the results you seek. The law of gratitude is the natural principle that action and reaction are always equal, and in opposite directions. The grateful outreaching of your mind in thankful praise to the Supreme is a liberation or expenditure of force; it cannot fail to reach that to which it addressed, and the reaction is an instantaneous movement towards you. "Draw nigh unto God, and He will draw nigh unto you." That is a statement of psychological truth.

And if your gratitude is strong and constant, the reaction in Formless Substance will be strong and continuous; the movement of the things you want will be always toward you. You cannot exercise much power without gratitude; for it is gratitude that keeps you connected with Power. But the value of gratitude does not consist solely in getting you more blessings in the future. Without gratitude you cannot long keep from dissatisfied thought regarding things as they are.

The moment you permit your mind to dwell with dissatisfaction upon things as they are, you begin to lose ground. You fix attention upon the common, the ordinary, the poor, and the squalid and mean; and your mind takes the form of these things. Then you will transmit these forms or mental images to the Formless, and the common, the poor, the squalid, and mean will come to you. To permit your mind to dwell upon the inferior is to become inferior and to surround yourself with inferior things. On the other hand, to fix your attention on the best is to surround yourself with the best, and to become the best.

The Creative Power within us makes us into the image of that to which we give our attention. We are Thinking Substance, and thinking substance always takes the form of that which it thinks about. The grateful mind is constantly fixed upon the best; therefore it tends to become the best; it takes the form or character of the best, and will receive the best.

Also, faith is born of gratitude. The grateful mind continually expects good things, and expectation becomes faith. The reaction of gratitude upon one's own mind produces faith; and every outgoing wave of grateful thanksgiving increases faith. He who has no feeling of gratitude cannot long retain a living faith; and without a living faith you cannot get rich by the creative method, as we shall see in the following chapters.

It is necessary, then, to cultivate the habit of being grateful for every good thing that comes to you; and to give thanks continuously. And because all things have contributed to your advancement, you should include all things in your gratitude. Do not waste time thinking or talking about the shortcomings or wrong actions of plutocrats or trust magnates. Their organization of the world has made your opportunity; all you get really comes to you because of them. Do not rage against, corrupt politicians; if it were not for politicians we should fall into anarchy, and your opportunity would be greatly lessened.

God has worked a long time and very patiently to bring us up to where we are in industry and government, and He is going right on with His work. There is not the least doubt that He will do away with plutocrats, trust magnates, captains of industry, and politicians as soon as they can be spared; but in the meantime, behold they are all very good. Remember that they are all helping to arrange the lines of transmission along which your riches will come to you, and be grateful to them all. This will bring you into harmonious relations with the good in everything, and the good in everything will move toward you.

CHAPTER 8 : Thinking in the Certain Way

TURN back to chapter 6 and read again the story of the man who formed a mental image of his house, and you will get a fair idea of the initial step toward getting rich. You must form a clear and definite mental picture of what you want; you cannot transmit an idea unless you have it yourself. You must have it before you can give it; and many people fail to impress Thinking Substance because they have themselves only a vague and misty concept of the things they want to do, to have, or to become.

It is not enough that you should have a general desire for wealth "to do good with"; everybody has that desire. It is not enough that you should have a wish to travel, see things, live more, etc. Everybody has those desires also. If you were going to send a wireless message to a friend, you would not send the letters of the alphabet in their order, and let him construct the message for himself; nor would you take words at random from the dictionary. You would send a coherent sentence; one which meant something. When you try to impress your wants upon Substance, remember that it must be done by a coherent statement; you must know what you want, and be definite. You can never get rich, or start the creative power into action, by sending out unformed longings and vague desires.

Go over your desires just as the man I have described went over his house; see just what you want, and get a clear mental picture of it as you wish it to look when you get it. That clear mental picture you must have continually in mind, as the sailor has in mind the port toward which he is sailing the ship; you must keep your face toward it all the time. You must no more lose sight of it than the steersman loses sight of the compass.

It is not necessary to take exercises in concentration, nor to set apart special times for prayer and affirmation, nor to "go into the silence," nor to do occult stunts of any kind. There things are well enough, but all you need is to know what you want, and to want it badly enough so that it will stay in your thoughts. Spend as much of your leisure time as you can in contemplating your picture, but no one needs to take exercises to concentrate his mind on a thing which he really wants; it is the things you do not really care about which require effort to fix your attention upon them.

And unless you really want to get rich, so that the desire is strong enough to hold your thoughts directed to the purpose as the magnetic pole holds the needle of the compass, it will hardly be worth while for you to try to carry out the instructions given in this book. The methods herein set forth are for people whose desire for riches is strong enough to overcome mental laziness and the love of ease, and make them work.

The more clear and definite you make your picture then, and the more you dwell upon it, bringing out all its delightful details, the stronger your desire will be; and the stronger your desire, the easier it will be to hold your mind fixed upon the picture of what you want.

Something more is necessary, however, than merely to see the picture clearly. If that is all you do, you are only a dreamer, and will have little or no power for accomplishment. Behind your clear vision must be the purpose to realize it; to bring it out in tangible expression. And behind this purpose must be an invincible and unwavering FAITH that the thing is already yours; that it is "at hand" and you have only to take possession of it.

Live in the new house, mentally, until it takes form around you physically. In the mental realm, enter at once into full enjoyment of the things you want. See the things you want as if they were actually around you all the time; see yourself as owning and using them. Make use of them in imagination just as you will use them when they are your tangible possessions. Dwell upon your mental picture until it is clear and distinct, and then take the Mental Attitude of Ownership toward everything in that picture. Take possession of it, in mind, in the full faith that it is actually yours. Hold to this mental ownership; do not waiver for an instant in the faith that it is real.

And remember what was said in a proceeding chapter about gratitude; be as thankful for it all the time as you expect to be when it has taken form. The man who can sincerely thank God for the things which as yet he owns only in imagination, has real faith. He will get rich; he will cause the creation of whatsoever he wants. You do not need to pray repeatedly for things you want; it is not necessary to tell God about it every day. Your part is to intelligently formulate your desire for the things which make for a larger life, and to get these desire arranged into a coherent whole; and then to impress this Whole Desire upon the Formless Substance, which has the power
and the will to bring you what you want.

You do not make this impression by repeating strings of words; you make it by holding the vision with unshakable PURPOSE to attain it, and with steadfast FAITH that you do attain it. The answer to prayer is not according to your faith while you are talking, but according to your faith while you are working. You cannot impress the mind of God by having a special Sabbath day set apart to tell Him what you want, and the forgetting Him during the rest of the week. You cannot impress Him by having special hours to go into your closet and pray, if you then dismiss the matter from your mind until the hour of prayer comes again.

Oral prayer is well enough, and has its effect, especially upon yourself, in clarifying your vision and strengthening your faith; but it is not your oral petitions which get you what you want. In order to get rich you do not need a "sweet hour of prayer"; you need to "pray without ceasing." And by prayer I mean holding steadily to your vision, with the purpose to cause its creation into solid form, and the faith that you are doing so. "Believe that ye receive them."

The whole matter turns on receiving, once you have clearly formed your vision. When you have formed it, it is well to make an oral statement, addressing the Supreme in reverent prayer; and from that moment you must, in mind, receive what you ask for. Live in the new house; wear the fine clothes; ride in the automobile; go on the journey, and confidently plan for greater journeys. Think and speak of all the things you have asked for in terms of actual present ownership. Imagine an environment, and a financial condition exactly as you want them, and live all the time in that imaginary environment and financial condition.

Mind, however, that you do not do this as a mere dreamer and castle builder; hold to the FAITH that the imaginary is being realized, and to the PURPOSE to realize it. Remember that it is faith and purpose in the use of the imagination which make the difference between the scientist and the dreamer. And having learned this fact, it is here that you must learn the proper use of the Will.

CHAPTER 9 : How to Use the Will

TO set about getting rich in a scientific way, you do not try to apply your will power to anything outside of yourself. Your have no right to do so, anyway. It is wrong to apply your will to other men and women, in order to get them to do what you wish done.

It is as flagrantly wrong to coerce people by mental power as it is to coerce them by physical power. If compelling people by physical force to do things for you reduces them to slavery, compelling them by mental means accomplishes exactly the same thing; the only difference is in methods. If taking things from people by physical force is robbery, thentaking things by mental force is robbery also; there is no difference in principle. You have no right to use your will power upon another person, even "for his own good"; for you do not know what is for his good. The science of getting rich does not require you to apply power or force to any other person, in any way whatsoever. There is not the slightest necessity for doing so; indeed, any attempt to use your will upon others will only tend to defeat your purpose. You do not need to apply your will to things, in order to compel them to come to you.

That would simply be trying to coerce God, and would be foolish and useless, as well as irreverent. You do not have to compel God to give you good things, any more than you have to use your will power to make the sun rise. You do not have to use your will power to conquer an unfriendly deity, or to make stubborn and rebellious forces do your bidding. Substance is friendly to you, and is more anxious to give you what you want than you are to get it. To get rich, you need only to use your will power upon yourself.

When you know what to think and do, then you must use your will to compel yourself to think and do the right things. That is the legitimate use of the will in getting what you want--to use it in holding yourself to the right course. Use your will to keep yourself thinking and acting in the Certain Way. Do not try to project your will, or your thoughts, or your mind out into space, to "act" on things or people. Keep your mind at home; it can accomplish more there than elsewhere. Use your mind to form a mental image of what you want, and to hold that vision with faith and purpose; and use your will to keep your mind working in the Right Way.

The more steady and continuous your faith and purpose, the more rapidly you will get rich, because you will make only POSITIVE impressions upon Substance; and you will not neutralize or offset them by negative impressions. The picture of your desires, held with faith and purpose, is taken up by the Formless, and permeates it to great distances-throughout the universe, for all I know.

As this impression spreads, all things are set moving toward its realization; every living thing, every inanimate thing, and the things yet uncreated, are stirred toward bringing into being that which you want. All force begins to be exerted in that direction; all things begin to move toward you. The minds of people, everywhere, are influenced toward doing the things necessary to the fulfilling of your desires; and they work for you, unconsciously.

But you can check all this by starting a negative impression in the Formless Substance. Doubt or unbelief is as certain to start a movement away from you as faith and purpose are to start one toward you. It is by not understanding this that most people who try to make use of "mental science" in getting rich make their failure. Every hour and moment you spend in giving heed to doubts and fears, every hour you spend in worry, every hour in which your soul is possessed by unbelief, sets a current away from you in the whole domain of intelligent Substance. All the promises are unto them that believe, and unto them only.

Since belief is all important, it behooves you to guard your thoughts; and as your beliefs will be shaped to a very great extent by the things you observe and think about, it is important that you should command your attention. And here the will comes into use; for it is by your will that you determine upon what things your attention shall be fixed.

If you want to become rich, you must not make a study of poverty. Things are not brought into being by thinking about their opposites. Health is never to be attained by studying disease and thinking about disease; righteousness is not to be promoted by studying sin and thinking about sin; and no one ever got rich by studying poverty and thinking about poverty. Medicine as a science of disease has increased disease; religion as a science of sin has promoted sin, and economics as a study of poverty will fill the world with wretchedness and want.

Do not talk about poverty; do not investigate it, or concern yourself with it. Never mind what its causes are; you have nothing to do with them. What

concerns you is the cure. Do not spend your time in charitable work, or charity movements; all charity
only tends to perpetuate the wretchedness it aims to eradicate. I do not say that you should be hard hearted or unkind, and refuse to hear the cry of need; but you must not try to eradicate poverty in any of the conventional ways. Put poverty behind you, and put all that pertains to it behind you, and "make good." Get rich; that is the best way you can help the poor.

And you cannot hold the mental image which is to make you rich if you fill your mind with pictures of poverty. Do not read books or papers which give circumstantial accounts of the wretchedness of the tenement dwellers, of the horrors of child labor, and so on. Do not read anything which fills your mind with gloomy images of want and suffering. You cannot help the poor in the least by knowing about these things; and the wide-spread knowledge of them does not tend at all to do away with poverty. What tends to do away with poverty is not the getting of pictures of poverty into your mind, but getting pictures of wealth into the minds of the poor.

You are not deserting the poor in their misery when you refuse to allow your mind to be filled with pictures of that misery. Poverty can be done away with, not by increasing the number of well to do people who think about poverty, but by increasing the number of poor people who purpose with faith to get rich. The poor do not need charity; they need inspiration. Charity only sends them a loaf of bread to keep them alive in their wretchedness, or gives them an entertainment to make them forget for an hour or two; but inspiration will cause them to rise out of their misery. If you want to help the poor, demonstrate to them that they can become rich; prove it by getting rich yourself.

The only way in which poverty will ever be banished from this world is by getting a large and constantly increasing number of people to practice the teachings of this book. People must be taught to become rich by creation, not by competition. Every man who becomes rich by competition throws down behind him the ladder by which he rises, and keeps others down; but every man who gets rich by creation opens a way for thousands to follow him, and inspires them to do so.

You are not showing hardness of heart or an unfeeling disposition when you refuse to pity poverty, see poverty, read about poverty, or think or talk about it, or to listen to those who do talk about it. Use your will power to keep your mind OFF the subject of poverty, and to keep it fixed with faith and purpose ON the vision of what you want.

CHAPTER 10 : Further Use of the Will

YOU cannot retain a true and clear vision of wealth if you are constantly turning your attention to opposing pictures, whether they be external or imaginary.

Do not tell of your past troubles of a financial nature, if you have had them, do not think of them at all. Do no tell of the poverty of your parents, or the hardships of your early life; to do any of these things is to mentally class yourself with the poor for the time being, and it will certainly check the movement of things in your direction.

Put poverty and all things that pertain to poverty completely behind you. You have accepted a certain theory of the universe as being correct, and are resting all your hopes of happiness on its being correct; and what can you gain by giving heed to conflicting theories? Do not read religious books which tell you that the world is soon coming to an end; and do not read the writing of muck-rakers and pessimistic philosophers who tell you that it is going to the devil.

The world is not going to the devil; it is going to God. It is wonderful Becoming.

True, there may be a good many things in existing conditions which are disagreeable; but what is the use of studying them when they are certainly passing away, and when the study of them only tends to check their passing and keep them with us? Why give time and attention to things which are being removed by evolutionary growth, when you can hasten their removal only by promoting the evolutionary growth as far as your part of it goes? No matter how horrible in seeming may be the conditions in certain countries, sections, or places, you waste your time and destroy your own chances by considering them.

You should interest yourself in the world's becoming rich. Think of the riches the world is coming into, instead of the poverty it is growing out of; and bear in mind that the only way in which you can assist the world in growing rich is by growing rich yourself through the creative method--not the competitive one. Give your attention wholly to riches; ignore poverty. Whenever you think or speak of those who are poor, think and speak of them as those who are becoming rich;as those who are to be congratulated rather than pitied. Then they and others will catch the inspiration, and begin to search for the way out.

41

Because I say that you are to give your whole time and mind and thought to riches, it does not follow that you are to be sordid or mean. To become really rich is the noblest aim you can have in life, for it includes everything else.

On the competitive plane, the struggle to get rich is a Godless scramble for power over other men; but when we come into the creative mind, all this is changed. All that is possible in the way of greatness and soul unfoldment, of service and lofty endeavor, comes by way of getting rich; all is made possible by the use of things. If you lack for physical health, you will find that the attainment of it is conditional on your getting rich. Only those who are emancipated from financial worry, and who have the means to live a care-free existence and follow hygienic practices, can have and retain health.

Moral and spiritual greatness is possible only to those who are above the competitive battle for existence; and only those who are becoming rich on the plane of creative thought are free from the degrading influences of competition. If your heart is set on domestic happiness, remember that love flourishes best where there is refinement, a high level of thought, and freedom from corrupting influences; and these are to be found only where riches are attained by the exercise of creative thought, without strife or rivalry. You can aim at nothing so great or noble, I repeat, as to become rich; and you must fix your attention upon your mental picture of riches, to the exclusion of all that may tend to dim or obscure the vision.

You must learn to see the underlying TRUTH in all things; you must see beneath all seemingly wrong conditions the Great One Life ever moving forward toward fuller expression and more complete happiness. It is the truth that there is no such thing as poverty; that there is only wealth. Some people remain in poverty because they are ignorant of the fact that there is wealth for them; and these can best be taught by showing them the way to affluence in your own person and practice.

Others are poor because, while they feel that there is a way out, they are too intellectually indolent to put forth the mental effort necessary to find that way And by travel it; and for these the very best thing you can do is to arouse their desire by showing them the happiness that comes from being rightly rich. Others still are poor because, while they have some notion of science, they have become so swamped and lost in the maze of metaphysical and occult theories that they do not know which road to take. They try a mixture of many systems and fail in all. For these, again, the very best thing, to do is to show the right way in your own person and practice; an ounce of doing things is worth a pound of theorizing. The very best thing you can do for the whole world is to make the most of yourself. You can serve God and man in no more effective way than by getting rich; that is, if you get rich by the creative method and not by the competetive one.

Another thing. We assert that this book gives in detail the principles of the science of getting rich; and if that is true, you do not need to read any other book upon the subject. This may sound narrow and egotistical, but consider: there is no more scientific method of computation in mathematics than by addition, subtraction, multiplication, and division; no other method is possible. There can be but one shortest distance between two points. There is only one way to think scientifically, and that is to think in the way that leads by the most direct and simple route to the goal. No man has yet formulated a briefer or less complex "system" than the one set forth herein; it has been stripped of all nonessential.

When you commence on this, lay all others aside; put them out of your mind altogether. Read this book every day; keep it with you; commit it to memory, and do not think about other "systems" and theories. If you do, you will begin to have doubts, and to be uncertain and wavering in your thought; and then you will begin to make failures.

After you have made good and become rich, you may study other systems as much as you please; but until you are quite sure that you have gained what you want, do not read anything on this line but this book, unless it be the authors mentioned in the Preface. And read only the most optimistic comments on the world's news; those in
Harmony with your picture.

Also, postpone your investigations into the occult. Do not dabble in theosophy, Spiritualism, or kindred studies. It is very likely that the dead still live, and are near; but if they are, let them alone; mind your own business. Wherever the spirits of the dead may be, they have their own work to do, and their own problems to solve; and we have no right to interfere with them. We cannot help them, and it is very doubtful whether they can help us, or whether we have any right to trespass upon their time if they can. Let the dead and the hereafter alone, and solve your own problem; get rich. If you begin to mix with the occult, you will start mental cross currents which will surely bring your hopes to shipwreck.

Now, this and the preceding chapters have brought us to the following statement of basic facts:

There is a thinking stuff from which all things are made, and which, in its original state, permeates, penetrates, and fills the interspaces of the universe. A thought, in this substance, produces the thing that is imaged by the thought. Man can form things in his thought, and, by impressing his thought upon formless substance, can cause the thing he thinks about to be created.

In order to do this, man must pass from the competitive to the creative mind; he must form a clear mental picture of the things he wants, and hold this picture in his thoughts with the fixed PURPOSE to get what he wants, and the unwavering FAITH that he does get what he wants, closing his mind against all that may tend to shake his purpose, dim his vision, or quench his faith. And in addition to all this, we shall now see that he must live and act in a Certain Way.

CHAPTER 11 : Acting in the Certain Way

THOUGHT is the creative power, or the impelling force which causes the creative power to act; thinking in a Certain Way will bring riches to you, but you must not rely upon thought alone, paying no attention to personal action. That is the rock upon which many otherwise scientific metaphysical thinkers meet shipwreck--the failure to connect thought with personal action.

We have not yet reached the stage of development, even supposing such a stage to be possible, in which man can create directly from Formless Substance without nature's processes or the work of human hands; man must not only think, but his personal action must supplement his thought. By thought you can cause the gold in the hearts of the mountains to be impelled toward you; but it will not mine itself, refine itself, coin itself into double eagles, and come rolling along the roads seeking its way into your pocket.

Under the impelling power of the Supreme Spirit, men's affairs will be so ordered that some one will be led to mine the gold for you; other men's business transactions will be so directed that the gold will be brought toward you, and you must so arrange your own business affairs that you may be able to receive it when it comes to you. Your thought makes all things, animate and inanimate, work to bring you what you want; but your personal activity must be such that you can rightly receive what you want when it reaches you. You are not to take it as charity, nor to steal it; you must give every man more in use value than he gives you in cash value.

The scientific use of thought consists in forming a clear and distinct mental image of what you want; in holding fast to the purpose to get what you want; and in realizing with grateful faith that you do get what you want. Do not try to 'project' your thought in any mysterious or occult way, with the idea of having it go out and do things for you; that is wasted effort, and will weaken your power to think with sanity.

The action of thought in getting rich is fully explained in the preceding chapters; your faith and purpose positively impress your vision upon Formless Substance, which has THE SAME DESIRE FOR MORE LIFE THAT YOU HAVE; and this vision, received from you, sets all the creative forces at work IN AND THROUGH THEIR REGULAR CHANNELS OF ACTION, but directed toward you.

It is not your part to guide or supervise the creative process; all you have to do with that is to retain your vision, stick to your purpose, and maintain your faith and gratitude.

But you must act in a Certain Way, so that you can appropriate what is yours when it comes to you; so that you can meet the things you have in your picture, and put them in their proper places as they arrive. You can really see the truth of this. When things reach you, they will be in the hands of other men, who will ask an equivalent for them. And you can only get what is yours by giving the other man what is his. Your pocketbook is not going to be transformed into a Fortunata's purse, which shall be always full of money without effort on your part.

This is the crucial point in the science of getting rich; right here, where thought and personal action must be combined. There are very many people who, consciously or unconsciously, set the creative forces in action by the strength and persistence of their desires, but who remain poor because they do not provide for the reception of the thing they want when it comes. By thought, the thing you want is brought to you; by action you receive it. Whatever your action is to be, it is evident that you must act NOW. You cannot act in the past, and it is essential to the clearness of your mental vision that you dismiss the past from your mind. You cannot act in the future, for the future is not here yet. And you cannot tell how you will want to act in any future contingency until that contingency has arrived.

Because you are not in the right business, or the right environment now, do not think that you must postpone action until you get into the right business or environment. And do not spend time in the present taking thought as to the best course in possible future emergencies; have faith in your ability to meet any emergency when it arrives. If you act in the present with your mind on the future, your present action will be with a divided mind, and will not be effective. Put your whole mind into present action.

Do not give your creative impulse to Original Substance, and then sit down and wait for results; if you do, you will never get them. Act now. There is never any time but now, and there never will be any time but now. If you are ever to begin to make ready for the reception of what you want, you must begin now. And your action, whatever it is, must most likely be in your present business or employment, and must be upon the persons and things in your present environment.

You cannot act where you are not; you cannot act where you have been, and you cannot act where you are going to be; you can act only where you are. Do not bother as to whether yesterday's work was well done or ill done; do today's work well. Do not try to do tomorrow's work now; there will be plenty of time to do that when you get to it. Do not try, by occult or mystical means, to act on people or things that are out of your reach. Do not wait for a change of environment, before you act; get a change of environment by action. You can so act upon the environment in which you are now, as to cause yourself to be transferred to a better environment. Hold with faith and purpose the vision of yourself in the better environment, but act upon your present environment with all your heart, and with all your strength, and with all your mind.

Do not spend any time in day dreaming or castle building; hold to the one vision of what you want, and act NOW. Do not cast about seeking some new thing to do, or some strange, unusual, or remarkable action to perform as a first step toward getting rich. It is probable that your actions, at least for some time to come, will be those you have been performing for some time past; but you are to begin now to perform these actions in the Certain Way, which will surely make you rich.

If you are engaged in some business, and feel that it is not the right one for you, do not wait until you get into the right business before you begin to act. Do not feel discouraged, or sit down and lament because you are misplaced. No man was ever so misplaced but that he could not find the right place, and no man ever became so involved in the wrong business but that he could get into the right business. Hold the vision of yourself in the right business, with the purpose to get into it, and the faith that you will get into it, and are getting into it; but ACT in your present business. Use your present business as the means of getting a better one, and use your present enviornment as the means of getting into a better one. Your vision of the right business, if held with faith and purpose, will cause the Supreme to move the right business toward you; and your action, if performed in the Certain Way, will cause you to move toward the business.

If you are an employee, or wage earner, and feel that you must change places in order to get what you want, do not 'project" your thought into space and rely upon it to get you another job. It will probably fail to do so. Hold the vision of yourself in the job you want, while you ACT with faith and purpose on the job you have, and you will certainly get the job you want. Your vision and faith will set the creative force in motion to bring it toward you, and your action will cause the forces in your own environment to move you toward the place you want.

In closing this chapter, we will add another statement to our syllabus: There is a thinking stuff from which all things are made, and which, in its original state, permeates, penetrates, and fills the interspaces of the universe.

A thought, in this substance, produces the thing that is imaged by the thought. Man can form things in his thought, and, by impressing his thought upon formless substance, can cause the thing he thinks about to be created. In order to do this, man must pass from the competitive to the creative mind; he must form a clear mental picture of the things he wants, and hold this picture in his thoughts with the fixed PURPOSE to get what he wants, and the unwavering FAITH that he does get what he wants, closing his mind to all that may tend to shake his purpose, dim his vision, or quench his faith. That he may receive what he wants when it comes, man must act NOW upon the people and things in his present environment.

CHAPTER 12 : Efficient Action

You must use your thought as directed in previous chapters, and begin to do what you can do where you are; and you must do ALL that you can do where you are.

You can advance only be being larger than your present place; and no man is larger than his present place who leaves undone any of the work pertaining to that place. The world is advanced only by those who more than fill their present places. If no man quite filled his present place, you can see that there must be a going backward in everything. Those who do not quite fill their present places are dead weight upon society, government, commerce, and industry; they must be carried along by others at a great expense. The progress of the world is retarded only by those who do not fill the places they are holding; they belong to a former age and a lower stage or plane of life, and their tendency is toward degeneration. No society could advance if every man was smaller than his place; social evolution is guided by the law of physical and mental evolution.

In the animal world, evolution is caused by excess of life. When an organism has more life than can be expressed in the functions of its own plane, it develops the organs of a higher plane, and a new species is originated. There never would have been new species had there not been organisms which more than filled their places.

The law is exactly the same for you; your getting rich depends upon your applying this principle to your own affairs. Every day is either a successful day or a day of failure; and it is the successful days which get you what you want. If everyday is a failure, you can never get rich; while if every day is a success, you cannot fail to get rich. If there is something that may be done today, and you do not do it, you have failed in so far as that thing is concerned; and the consequences may be more disastrous than you imagine.

You cannot foresee the results of even the most trivial act; you do not know the workings of all the forces that have been set moving in your behalf. Much may be depending on your doing some simple act; it may be the very thing which is to open the door of opportunity to very great possibilities. You can never know all the combinations which Supreme Intelligence is making for you in the world of things and of things and of human affairs; your neglect or failure to do some small thing may cause a long delay in getting what you want.

Do, every day, ALL that can be done that day.

There is, however, a limitation or qualification of the above that you must take into account. You are not to overwork, nor to rush blindly into your business in the effort to do the greatest possible number of things in the shortest possible time. You are not to try to do tomorrow's work today, nor to do a week's work in a day. It is really not he number of things you do, but the EFFICIENCY of each separate action that counts.

Every act is, in itself, either a success or a failure.

Every act is, in itself, either effective or inefficient.

Every inefficient act is a failure, and if you spend your life in doing inefficient acts, your whole life will be a failure.

The more things you do, the worse for you, if all your acts are inefficient ones. On the other hand, every efficient act is a success in itself, and if every act of your life is an efficient one, your whole life MUST be a success.

The cause of failure is doing too many things in an inefficient manner, and not doing enough things in an efficient manner. You will see that it is a self-evident proposition that if you do not do any inefficient acts, and if you do a sufficient number of efficient acts, you will become rich. If, now, it is possible for you to make each act an efficient one, you see again that the getting of riches is reduced to an exact science, like mathematics.

The matter turns, then, on the questions whether you can make each separate act a success in itself. And this you can certainly do. You can make each act a success, because ALL Power is working with you; and ALL Power cannot fail. Power is at your service; and to make each act efficient you have only to put power into it.

Every action is either strong or weak; and when every one is strong, you are acting in the Certain Way which will make you rich. Every act can be made strong and efficient by holding your vision while you are doing it, and putting the whole power of your FAITH and PURPOSE into it.

It is at this point that the people fail who separate mental power from personal action. They use the power of mind in one place and at one time, and they act in another pace and at another time. So their acts are not successful in themselves; too many of them are inefficient. But if ALL Power goes into every act, no matter how commonplace, every act will be a success in itself; and as in the nature of things every success opens the way to other successes, your progress toward what you want, and the progress of what you want toward you, will become increasingly rapid.

Remember that successful action is cumulative in its results. Since the desire for more life is inherent in all things, when a man begins to move toward larger life more things attach themselves to him, and the influence of his desire is multiplied. Do, every day, all that you can do that day, and do each act in an efficient manner.

In saying that you must hold your vision while you are doing each act, however trivial or commonplace, I do not mean to say that it is necessary at all times to see the vision distinctly to its smallest details. It should be the work of your leisure hours to use your imagination on the details of your vision, and to contemplate them until they are firmly fixed upon memory. If you wish speedy results, spend practically all your spare time in this practice. By continuous contemplation you will get the picture of what you want, even to the smallest details, so firmly fixed upon your mind, and so completely transferred to the mind of Formless Substance, that in your working hours you need only to mentally refer to the picture to stimulate your faith and purpose, and cause your best effort to be put forth.

Contemplate your picture in your leisure hours until your consciousness is so full of it that you can grasp it instantly. You will become so enthused with its bright promises that the mere thought of it will call forth the strongest energies of your whole being.

Let us again repeat our syllabus, and by slightly changing the closing statements bring it to the point we have now reached.

There is a thinking stuff from which all things are made, and which, in its original state, permeates, penetrates, and fills the interspaces of the universe. A thought, in this substance, Produces the thing that is imaged by the thought. Man can form things in his thought, and, by impressing his thought upon formless substance, can cause the thing he thinks about to be created. In order to do this, man must pass from the competitive to the creative mind; he must form a clear mental picture of the things he wants, and do, with faith and purpose, all that can be done each day, doing each separate thing in an efficient manner.

CHAPTER 13 : Getting into the Right Business

SUCCESS, in any particular business, depends for one thing upon your possessing in a well-developed state the faculties required in that business. Without good musical faculty no one can succeed as a teacher of music; without well-developed mechanical faculties no one can achieve great success in any of the mechanical trades; without tact and the commercial faculties no one can succeed in mercantile pursuits. But to possess in a well-developed state the faculties required in your particular vocation does not insure getting rich. There are musicians who have remarkable talent, and who yet remain poor; there are blacksmiths, carpenters, and so on who have excellent mechanical ability, but who do not get rich; and there are merchants with good faculties for dealing with men who nevertheless fail.

The different faculties are tools; it is essential to have good tools, but it is also essential that the tools should be used in the Right Way. One man can take a sharp saw, a square, a good plane, and so on, and build a handsome article of furniture; another man can take the same tools and set to work to duplicate the article, but his production will be a botch. He does not know how to use good tools in a successful way.

The various faculties of your mind are the tools with which you must do the work which is to make you rich; it will be easier for you to succeed if you get into a business for which you are well equipped with mental tools. Generally speaking, you will do best in that business which will use your strongest faculties; the one for which you are naturally "best fitted." But there are limitations to this statement, also. No man should regard his vocation as being irrevocably fixed by the tendencies with which he was born.

You can get rich in ANY business, for if you have not the right talent for you can develop that talent; it merely means that you will have to make your tools as you go along, instead of confining yourself to the use of those with which you were born. It will be EASIER for you to succeed in a vocation for which you already have the talents in a well-developed state; but you CAN succeed in any vocation, for you can develop any rudimentary talent, and there is no talent of which you have not at least the rudiment.

You will get rich most easily in point of effort, if you do that for which you are best fitted; but you will get rich most satisfactorily if you do that which you WANT to do.

Doing what you want to do is life; and there is no real satisfaction in living if we are compelled to be forever doing something which we do not like to do, and can never do what we want to do. And it is certain that you can do what you want to do; the desire to do it is proof that you have within you the power which can do it.

Desire is a manifestation of power. The desire to play music is the power which can play music seeking expression and development; the desire to invent mechanical devices is the mechanical talent seeking expression and development. Where there is no power, either developed or undeveloped, to do a thing, there is never any desire to do that thing; and where there is strong desire to do a thing, it is certain proof that the power to do it is strong, and only requires to be developed and applied in the Right Way.

All things else being equal, it is best to select the business for which you have the best developed talent; but if you have a strong desire to engage in any particular line of work, you should select that work as the ultimate end at which you aim. You can do what you want to do, and it is your right and privilege to follow the business or a vocation which will be most congenial and pleasant. You are not obliged to do what you do not like to do, and should not do it except as a means to bring you to the doing of the thing you want to do.

If there are past mistakes whose consequences have placed you in an undesirable business or environment, you may be obliged for some time to do what you do not like to do; but you can make the doing of it pleasant by knowing that it is making it possible for you to come to the doing of what you want to do. If you feel that you are not in the right vocation, do not act too hastily in trying to get into another one. The best way, generally, to change business or environment is by growth. Do not be afraid to make a sudden and radical change if the opportunity is presented, and you feel after careful consideration that it is the right opportunity; but never take sudden or radical action when you are in doubt as to the wisdom of doing so. There is never any hurry on the creative plane; and there is no lack of opportunity.

When you get out of the competitive mind you will understand that you never need to act hastily. No one else is going to beat you to the thing you want to do; there is enough for all. If one space is taken, another and a better one will be opened for you a little farther on; there is plenty of time. When you are in doubt, wait. Fall back on the contemplation of your vision, and increase your faith and purpose; and by all means, in times of doubt and indecision, cultivate gratitude.

A day or two spent in contemplating the vision of what you want, and in earnest thanksgiving that you are getting it, will bring your mind into such close relationship with the Supreme that you will make no mistake when you do act. There is a mind which knows all there is to know; and you can come into close unity with this mind by faith and the purpose to advance in life, if you have deep gratitude.

Mistakes come from acting hastily, or from acting in fear or doubt, or in forgetfulness of the Right Motive, which is more life to all, and less to none. As you go on in the Certain Way, opportunities will come to you in increasing number; and you will need to be very steady in your faith and purpose, and to keep in close touch with the All Mind by reverent gratitude. Do all that you can do in a perfect manner every day, but do it without haste, worry, or fear. Go as fast as you can, but never hurry.

Remember that in the moment you begin to hurry you cease to be a creator and become a competitor; you drop back upon the old plane again. Whenever you find yourself hurrying, call a halt; fix your attention on the mental image of the thing you want, and begin to give thanks that you are getting it. The exercise of GRATITUDE will never fail to strengthen your faith and renew your purpose.

CHAPTER 14 : The Impression of Increase

WHETHER you change your vocation or not, your actions for the present must be those pertaining to the business in which you are now engaged. You can get into the business you want by making constructive use of the business you are already established in; by doing your daily work in a Certain Way.

And in so far as your business consists in dealing with other men, whether personally or by letter, the key-thought of all your efforts must be to convey to their minds the impression of increase. Increase is what all men and all women are seeking; it is the urge of the Formless Intelligence within them, seeking fuller expression.

The desire for increase is inherent in all nature; it is the fundamental impulse of the universe. All human activities are based on the desire for increase; people are seeking more food, more clothes, better shelter, more luxury, more beauty, more knowledge, more pleasure-- increase in something, more life. Every living thing is under this necessity for continuous advancement; where increase of life ceases, dissolution and death set in at once. Man instinctively knows this, and hence he is forever seeking more. The normal desire for increased wealth is not an evil or a reprehensible thing; it
is simply the desire for more abundant life; it is aspiration. And because it is the deepest instinct of their natures, all men and women are attracted to him who can give them more of the means of life.

In following the Certain Way as described in the foregoing pages, you are getting continuous increase for yourself, and you are giving it to all with whom you deal. You are a creative center, from which increase is given off to all. Be sure of this, and convey assurance of the fact to every man, woman, and child with whom you come in contact. No matter how small the transaction, even if it be only the selling of a stick of candy to a little child, put into it the thought of increase, and make sure that the customer is impressed with the thought.

Convey the impression of advancement with everything you do, so that all people shall receive the impression that you are an Advancing Man, and that you advance all who deal with you. Even to the people whom you meet in a social way, without any thought of business, and to whom you do not try to sell anything, give the thought of increase. You can convey this impression by holding the unshakable faith that you, yourself, are in the Way of Increase; and by letting this faith inspire, fill, and permeate every action.

Do everything that you do in the firm conviction that you are an advancing personality, and that you are giving advancement to everybody. Feel that you are getting rich, and that in so doing you are making others rich, and conferring benefits on all.

Do not boast or brag of your success, or talk about it unnecessarily; true faith is never boastful. Wherever you find a boastful person, you find one who is secretly doubtful and afraid. Simply feel the faith, and let it work out in every transaction; let every act and tone and look express the quiet assurance that you are getting rich; that you are already rich. Words will not be necessary to communicate this feeling to others; they will feel the sense of increase when in your presence, and will be attracted to you again.

You must so impress others that they will feel that in associating with you they will get increase for themselves. See that you give them a use value greater than the cash value you are taking from them. Take an honest pride in doing this, and let everybody know it; and you will have no lack of customers. People will go where they are given increase; and the Supreme, which desires increase in all, and which knows all, will move toward you men and women who have never heard of you. Your business will increase rapidly, and you will be surprised at the unexpected benefits which will come to you. You will be able from day to day to make larger combinations, secure greater advantages, and to go on into a more congenial vocation if you desire to do so.

But doing thing all this, you must never lose sight of your vision of what you want, or your faith and purpose to get what you want. Let me here give you another word of caution in regard to motives. Beware of the insidious temptation to seek for power over other men. Nothing is so pleasant to the unformed or partially developed mind as the exercise of power or dominion over others. The desire to rule for selfish gratification has been the curse of the world. For countless ages kings and lords have drenched the earth with blood in their battles to extend their dominions; this not to seek more life for all, but to get more power for themselves.

Today, the main motive in the business and industrial world is the same; men Marshal their armies of dollars, and lay waste the lives and hearts of millions in the same mad scramble for power over others. Commercial kings, like political kings, are inspired by the lust for power. Look out for the temptation to seek for authority, to become a "master," to be considered as one who is above the common herd, to impress others by lavish display, and so on. The mind that seeks for mastery over others is the competitive mind; and the competitive mind is not the creative one. In order to master your environment and your destiny, it is not at all necessary that you should rule over your fellow men and indeed, when you fall into the world's struggle for the high places, you begin to be conquered by fate and environment, and your getting rich becomes a matter of chance and speculation.

Beware of the competitive mind!! No better statement of the principle of creative action can be formulated than the favorite declaration of the late "Golden Rule" Jones of Toledo: "What I want for myself, I want for everybody."

CHAPTER 15 : The Advancing Man

WHAT I have said in the last chapter applies as well to the professional man and the wage-earner as to the man who is engaged in mercantile business. No matter whether you are a physician, a teacher, or a clergyman, if you can give increase of life to others and make them sensible of the fact, they will be attracted to you, and you will get rich. The physician who holds the vision of himself as a great and successful healer, and who works toward the complete realization of that vision with faith and purpose, as described in former chapters, will come into such close touch with the Source of Life that he will be phenomenally successful; patients will come to him in throngs.

No one has a greater opportunity to carry into effect the teaching of this book than the practitioner of medicine; it does not matter to which of the various schools he may belong, for the principle of healing is common to all of them, and may be reached by all alike. The Advancing Man in medicine, who holds to a clear mental image of himself as successful, and who obeys the laws of faith, purpose, and gratitude, will cure every curable case he undertakes, no matter what remedies he may use. In the field of religion, the world cries out for the clergyman who can teach his hearers the true science of abundant life. He who masters the details of the science of getting rich, together with the allied sciences of being well, of being great, and of winning love, and who teaches these details from the pulpit, will never lack for a congregation. This is the gospel that the world needs; it will give increase of life, and men will hear it gladly, and will give liberal support to the man who brings it to them.

What is now needed is a demonstration of the science of life from the pulpit. We want preachers who can not only tell us how, but who in their own persons will show us how. We need the preacher who will himself be rich, healthy, great, and beloved, to teach us how to attain to these things; and when he comes he will find a numerous and loyal following. The same is true of the teacher who can inspire the children with the faith and purpose of the advancing life. He will never be "out of a job." And any teacher who has this faith and purpose can give it to his pupils; he cannot help giving it to them if it is part of his own life and practice.

What is true of the teacher, preacher, and physician is true of the lawyer, dentist, real estate man, insurance agent--of everybody. The combined mental and personal action I have described is infallible; it cannot fail. Every man and woman who follows these instructions steadily, perseveringly, and to the letter, will get rich. The law of the Increase of Life is as mathematically certain in its operation as the law of gravitation; getting rich is an exact science.

The wage earner will find this as true of his case as of any of the others mentioned. Do not feel that you have no chance to get rich because you are working where there is no visible opportunity for advancement, where wages are small and the cost of living high. Form your clear mental vision of what you want, and begin to act with faith and purpose.

Do all the work you can do, every day, and do each piece of work in a perfectly successful manner; put the power of success, and the purpose to get rich, into everything that you do. But do not do this merely with the idea of currying favor with your employer, in the hope that he, or those above you, will see your good work and advance you; it is not likely that they will do so. The man who is merely a "good" workman, filling his place to the very best of his ability, and satisfied with that, is valuable to his employer; and it is not to the employer's interest to promote him; he is worth more where he is.

To secure advancement, something more is necessary than to be too large for your place. The man who is certain to advance is the one who is too big for his place, and who has a clear concept of what he wants to be; who knows that he can become what he wants to be and who is determined to BE what he wants to be. Do not try to more than fill your present place with a view to pleasing your employer; do it with the idea of advancing yourself. Hold the faith and purpose of increase during work hours, after work hours, and before work hours. Hold it in such a way that every person who comes in contact with you, whether foreman, fellow workman, or social acquaintance, will feel the power of purpose radiating from you; so that every one will get the sense of advancement and increase from you. Men will be attracted to you, and if there is no possibility for advancement in your present job, you will very soon see an opportunity to take another job.

There is a Power which never fails to present opportunity to the Advancing Man who is moving in obedience to law. God cannot help helping you, if you act in a Certain Way; He must do so in order to help Himself. There is nothing in your circumstances or in the industrial situation that can keep you down. If you cannot get rich working for the steel trust, you can get rich on a ten-acre farm; and if you begin to move in the Certain Way, you will certainly escape from the "clutches" of the steel trust and get on to the farm or wherever else you wish to be.

If a few thousands of its employees would enter upon the Certain Way, the steel trust would soon be in a bad plight; it would have to give its workingmen more opportunity, or go out of business. Nobody has to work for a trust; the trusts can keep men in so called hopeless conditions only so long as there are men who are too ignorant to know of the science of getting rich, or too intellectually slothful to practice it.

Begin this way of thinking and acting, and your faith and purpose will make you quick to see any opportunity to better your condition. Such opportunities will speedily come, for the Supreme, working in All, and working for you, will bring them before you. Do not wait for an opportunity to be all that you want to be; when an opportunity to be more than you are now is presented and you feel impelled toward it, take it. It will be the first step toward a greater opportunity. There is no such thing possible in this universe as a lack of opportunities for the man who is living the advancing life.

It is inherent in the constitution of the cosmos that all things shall be for him and work together for his good; and he must certainly get rich if he acts and thinks in the Certain Way. So let wage-earning men and women study this book with great care, and enter with confidence upon the course of action it prescribes; it will not fail.

CHAPTER 16 : Some Cautions, and Concluding Observations

MANY people will scoff at the idea that there is an exact science of getting rich; holding the impression that the supply of wealth is limited, they will insist that social and governmental institutions must be changed before even any considerable number of people can acquire a competence.

But this is not true.

It is true that existing governments keep the masses in poverty, but this is because the masses do not think and act in the Certain Way. If the masses begin to move forward as suggested in this book, neither governments nor industrial systems can check them; all systems must be modified to accommodate the forward movement. If the people have the Advancing Mind, have the Faith that they can become rich, and move forward with the fixed purpose to become rich, nothing can possibly keep them in poverty.

Individuals may enter upon the Certain Way at any time, and under any government, and make themselves rich; and when any considerable number of individuals do so under any government, they will cause the system to be so modified as to open the way for others. The more men who get rich on the competitive plane, the worse for others; the more who get rich on the creative plane, the better for others. The economic salvation of the masses can only be accomplished by getting a large number of people to practice the scientific method set down in this book, and become rich. These will show others the way, and inspire them with a desire for real life, with the faith that it can be attained, and with the purpose to attain it.

For the present, however, it is enough to know that neither the government under which you live nor the capitalistic or competitive system of industry can keep you from getting rich. When you enter upon the creative plane of thought you will rise above all these things and become a citizen of another kingdom. But remember that your thought must be held upon the creative plane; you are never for an instant to be betrayed into regarding the supply as limited, or into acting on the moral level of competition.

Whenever you do fall into old ways of thought, correct yourself instantly; for when you are in the competitive mind, you have lost the cooperation of the

Mind of the Whole. Do not spend any time in planning as to how you will meet possible emergencies in the future, except as the necessary policies may affect your actions today. You are concerned with doing today's work in a perfectly successful manner, and not with emergencies which may arise tomorrow; you can attend to them as they come.

Do not concern yourself with questions as to how you shall surmount obstacles which may loom upon your business horizon, unless you can see plainly that your course must be altered today in order to avoid them. No matter how tremendous an obstruction may appear at a distance, you will find that if you go on in the Certain Way it will disappear as you approach it, or that a way over, though, or around it will appear. No possible combination of circumstances can defeat a man or woman who is
proceeding to get rich along strictly scientific lines. No man or woman who obeys the law can fail to get rich, any more than one can multiply two by two and fail to get four.

Give no anxious thought to possible disasters, obstacles, panics, or unfavorable combinations of circumstances; it is time enough to meet such things when they present themselves before you in the immediate present, and you will find that every difficulty carries with it the wherewithal for its overcoming.

Guard your speech. Never speak of yourself, your affairs, or of anything else in a discouraged or discouraging way. Never admit the possibility of failure, or speak in a way that infers failure as a possibility. Never speak of the times as being hard, or of business conditions as being doubtful. Times may be hard and business doubtful for those who are on the competitive plane, but they can never be so for you; you can create what you want, and you are above fear. When others are having hard times and poor business, you will find your greatest opportunities.

Train yourself to think of and to look upon the world as a something which is Becoming, which is growing; and to regard seeming evil as being only that which is undeveloped. Always speak in terms of advancement; to do otherwise is to deny your faith, and to deny your faith is to lose it. Never allow yourself to feel disappointed. You may expect to have a certain thing at a certain time, and not get it at that time; and this will appear to you like failure. But if you hold to your faith you will find that the failure is only apparent. Go on in the certain way, and if you do not receive that thing, you will receive something so much better that you will see that the seeming failure was really a great success.

63

A student of this science had set his mind on making a certain business combination which seemed to him at the time to be very desirable, and he worked for some, weeks to bring it about. When the crucial time came, the thing failed in a perfectly inexplicable way; it was as if some unseen influence had been working secretly against him. He was not disappointed; on the contrary, he thanked God that his desire had been overruled, and went steadily on with a grateful mind. In a few weeks an opportunity so much better came his way that he would not have made the first deal on any account; and he saw that a Mind which knew more than he knew had prevented him from losing the greater good by entangling himself with the lesser

.

That is the way every seeming failure will work out for you, if you keep your faith, hold to your purpose, have gratitude, and do, every day, all that can be done that day, doing each separate act in a successful manner. When you make a failure, it is because you have not asked for enough; keep on, and a larger thing then you were seeking will certainly come to you. Remember this.

You will not fail because you lack the necessary talent to do what you wish to do. If you go on as I have directed, you will develop all the talent that is necessary to the doing of your work. It is not within the scope of this book to deal with the science of cultivating talent; but it is as certain and simple as the process of getting rich. However, do not hesitate or waver for fear that when you come to any certain place you will fail for lack of ability; keep right on, and when you come to that place, the ability will be furnished to you. The same source of Ability which enabled the untaught Lincoln to do the greatest work in government ever accomplished by a single man is open to you; you may draw upon all the mind there is for wisdom to use in meeting the responsibilities which are laid upon you.

Go on in full faith. Study this book. Make it your constant companion until you have mastered all the ideas contained in it. While you are getting firmly established in this faith, you will do well to give up most recreations and pleasure; and to stay away from places where ideas conflicting with these are advanced in lectures or sermons. Do not read pessimistic or conflicting literature, or get into arguments upon the matter. Do very little reading, outside of the writers mentioned in the Preface. Spend most of your leisure time in contemplating your vision, and in cultivating gratitude, and in reading this book. It contains all you need to know of the science of getting rich; and you will find all the essentials summed up in the following chapter.

CHAPTER 17 : Summary of the Science of Getting Rich

THERE is a thinking stuff from which all things are made, and which, in its original state, permeates, penetrates, and fills the interspaces of the universe. A thought in this substance produces the thing that is imaged by the thought. Man can form things in his thought, and by impressing his thought upon formless substance can cause the thing he thinks about to be created.

In order to do this, man must pass from the competitive to the creative mind; otherwise he cannot be in harmony with the Formless Intelligence, which is always creative and never competitive in spirit.

Man may come into full harmony with the Formless Substance by entertaining a lively and sincere gratitude for the blessings it bestows upon him. Gratitude unifies the mind of man with the intelligence of Substance, so that man's thoughts are received by the Formless. Man can remain upon the creative plane only by uniting himself with the Formless Intelligence through a deep and continuous feeling of gratitude.

Man must form a clear and definite mental image of the things he wishes to have, to do, or to become; and he must hold this mental image in his thoughts, while being deeply grateful to the Supreme that all his desires are granted to him. The man who wishes to get rich must spend his leisure hours in contemplating his Vision, and in earnest thanksgiving that the reality is being given to him. Too much stress cannot be laid on the importance of frequent contemplation of the mental image, coupled with unwavering faith and devout gratitude. This is the process by which the impression is given to the Formless, and the creative forces set in motion.

The creative energy works through the established channels of natural growth, and of the industrial and social order. All that is included in his mental image will surely be brought to the man who follows the instructions given above, and whose faith does not waver. What he wants will come to him through the ways of established trade and commerce.

In order to receive his own when it shall come to him, man must be active; and this activity can only consist in more than filling his present place. He must keep in mind the Purpose to get rich through the realization of his mental image. And he must do, every day, all that can be done that day, taking care to do each act in a successful manner. He must give to every man a use value in excess of the cash value he receives, so that each transaction makes for more life; and he must so hold the Advancing Thought that the impression of increase will be communicated to all with whom he comes in contact. The men and women who practice the foregoing instructions will certainly get rich; and the riches they receive will be in exact proportion to the definiteness of their vision, the fixity of their purpose, the steadiness of their faith, and the depth of their gratitude.

THE END

The Master Key System
By Charles Haanel

CONTENTS

BEFORE WE BEGIN: CHARLES HAANEL
Before We Begin: Charles Haanel Biography

Charles F. Haanel was a noted American author and businessman who belonged to the American Scientific League, The Author's League of America, The American Society of Psychical Research, the St. Louis Humane Society and the St. Louis Chamber of Commerce.

Born in Ann Arbor, Michigan, Charles F. Haanel began his business career in St. Louis. He resigned his position in order to start his own company and eventually founded one of the largest conglomerates of his time.

He wrote several books which were published in St. Louis by Psychology Publishing and by his Master Key Institute in New York. Mr. Haanel put into books the ideas and methods he used to gain his success. Besides the "Master Key System", he also wrote "Mental Chemistry" and "The New Psychology"

The Master Key System had sold over 200,000 copies and then seemingly disappeared. The Master Key System is one of the finest studies in self-improvement and higher consciousness ever written. Covering everything from how to get wealthy to how to get healthy, Mr. Haanel leaves no stone unturned. With precision, he elucidates on each topic with logic and rigor that not only leaves you feeling good, but also thinking good. The book was banned by the Church and has been hidden away for seventy years!

Rumor has it that while he was attending Harvard University, Bill Gates discovered and read The Master Key System by Charles F. Haanel. It was this book that inspired Bill Gates to drop out of the University and pursue his dream of "a computer on every desktop." You probably know the results. . .

It is Silicon Valley's secret that almost every entrepreneur who made a fortune in recent years did so by studying the words Mr. Haanel penned over eighty years ago! Almost every millionaire and billionaire in the Valley read The Master Key System by Charles F. Haanel. Since this book was no longer in print until recently, copies of The Master Key System became a hot commodity in the Valley.

The Master Key System is a system that teaches the ultimate principles, causes, effects, and laws that underlie all attainment and success. When you want to attain something, The Master Key System will show you how to get it. The results you will attain from using this system are so startling as to appear incredible. For this reason, more and more people are becoming students of The Master Key System than ever before

In 24 parts, The Master Key sets out the fundamental principles of life and creative living, as Haanel came to understand and apply them. Basic to his teaching is the correct development and use of mental power -- the key to truly creative power and action, harmony and health, love and happiness, and abundant possibilities. Each part is meant to be studied like a correspondence course lesson, but this is also a book that can be opened at random for whatever gem of advice your eyes happen to fall upon.

This age-old wisdom was written by someone who could perceive and tap into Universal Mind but who seems to have no particular allegiance to any specific system of knowledge. Haanel's numbered, common-sense messages still have a freshness 89 years after they were first assembled.

Walter B. Stevens described Mr. Haanel as "a man of mature judgment, capable of taking a calm survey of life and correctly valuing its opportunities, its possibilities, its demands and obligations."

INTRODUCTION

Nature compels us all to move through life. We could not remain stationary however much we wished. Every right-thinking person wants not merely to move through life like a sound-producing, perambulating plant, but to develop - to improve - and to continue the development mentally to the close of physical life.

This development can occur only through the improvement of the quality of individual thought, and the ideals, actions and conditions that arise as a consequence. Hence a study of the creative processes of thought and how to apply them is of supreme importance to each one of us. This knowledge is the means whereby the evolution of human life on earth may be hastened and uplifted in the process.

Humanity ardently seeks "The Truth" and explores every avenue to it. In this process it has produced a special literature, which ranges the whole gamut of thought from the trivial to the sublime - up from Divination, through all the Philosophies, to the final lofty Truth of "The Master Key".

The "Master Key" is here given to the world as a means of tapping the great cosmic intelligence and attracting from it that which corresponds to the ambitions and aspirations of each reader.

Every thing and institution we see around us, created by human agency, had first to exist as a thought in some human mind. Thought, therefore, is constructive. Human thought is the spiritual power of the cosmos operating through its creature man. "The Master Key" instructs the reader how to use that power, and use it both constructively and creatively. The things and conditions we desire to become realities we must first create in thought. "The Master Key" explains and guides the process.

"The Master Key" teaching has hitherto been published in the form of a Correspondence Course of 24 lessons, delivered to students one per week for 24 weeks. The reader, who now receives the whole 24 parts at one time, is warned not to attempt to read the book like a novel, but to treat it as a course of study and conscientiously to imbibe the meaning of each part - reading and re-reading one part only per week before proceeding to the next. Otherwise, the later parts will tend to be misunderstood and the reader's time and money will be wasted.

Used as thus instructed, "The Master Key" will make of the reader a greater, better personality, and equipped with a new power to achieve any worthy personal purpose and a new ability to enjoy life's beauty and wonder.

F.H. BURGESS
FOREWORD

Some men seem to attract success, power, wealth, attainment, with very little conscious effort; others conquer with great difficulty; still others fail altogether to reach their ambitions, desires and ideals. Why is this so? Why should some men realize their ambitions easily, others with difficulty, and still others not at all? The cause cannot be physical, else the most perfect men, physically, would be the most successful. The difference, therefore, must be mental - must be in the mind; hence mind must be the creative force, must constitute the sole difference between men. It is mind, therefore, which overcomes environment and every other obstacle in the path of men.

When the creative power of thought is fully understood, its effect will be seen to be marvelous. But such results cannot be secured without proper application, diligence, and concentration. The student will find that the laws governing in the mental and spiritual world are as fixed and infallible as in the material world. To secure the desired results, then, it is necessary to know the law and to comply with it. A proper compliance with the law will be found to produce the desired result with invariable exactitude. The student who learns that power comes from within, that he is weak only because he has depended on help from outside, and who unhesitatingly throws himself on his own thought, instantly rights himself, stands erect, assumes a dominant attitude, and works miracles.

It is evident, therefore, that he who fails to fully investigate and take advantage of the wonderful progress which is being made in this last and greatest science, will soon be as far behind as the man who would refuse to acknowledge and accept the benefits which have accrued to mankind through an understanding of the laws of electricity.

Of course, mind creates negative conditions just as readily as favorable conditions, and when we consciously or unconsciously visualize every kind of lack, limitation and discord, we create these conditions; this is what many are unconsciously doing all the time.

This law as well as every other law is no respecter of persons, but is in constant operation and is relentlessly bringing to each individual exactly what he has created; in other words, "Whatsoever a man soweth that shall he also reap."

Abundance, therefore, depends upon a recognition of the laws of Abundance, and the fact that Mind is not only the creator, but the only creator of all there is. Certainly nothing can be created before we know that it can be created and then make the proper effort. There is no more electricity in the world today than there was fifty years ago, but until someone recognized the law by which it could be made of service, we received no benefit; now that the law is understood, practically the whole world is lit by it. So with the law of Abundance; it is only those who recognize the law and place themselves in harmony with it who share in its benefits.

The scientific spirit now dominates every field of effort; relations of cause and effect are no longer ignored.

The discovery of a region of law marked an epoch in human progress. It eliminated the element of uncertainty and caprice in men's lives, and substituted law, reason and certitude.

Men now understand that for every result there is an adequate and definite cause, so that when a given result is desired, they seek the condition by which alone this result may be attained.

The basis upon which all law rests was discovered by inductive reasoning, which consists of comparing a number of separate instances with one another until the common factor which gives rise to them all is seen.

It is this method of study to which the civilized nations owe the greater part of their prosperity and the more valuable part of their knowledge. It has lengthened life, it has mitigated pain, it has spanned rivers, it has brightened the night with the splendor of day, extended the range of vision, accelerated motion, annihilated distance, facilitated intercourse, and enabled men to descend into the sea and into the air. What wonder then that men soon endeavored to extend the blessings of this system of study to their method of thinking, so that when it became plainly evident that certain results followed a particular method of thinking, it only remained to classify these results.

This is method is scientific, and it is the only method by which we shall be permitted to retain that degree of liberty and freedom which we have been accustomed to look upon as an inalienable right; because a people is safe at home and in the world only if national preparedness mean such things as growing surplus of health, accumulated efficiency in public and private business of whatever sort, continuous advance in the science and art of acting together, and the increasingly dominant endeavor to make all of these and all other aspects of national development center and revolve about ascending life, single and collective, for which science, art and ethics furnish guidance and controlling motives.

The Master Key is based on absolute scientific truth and will unfold the possibilities that lie dormant in the individual and teach how they may be brought into powerful action to increase the person's effective capacity, bringing added energy, discernment, vigor and mental elasticity. The student who gains an understanding of the mental laws which are unfolded will come into the possession of an ability to secure results hitherto undreamed of, and rewards hardly to be expressed in words.

It explains the correct use of both the receptive and active elements of the mental nature, and instructs the student in the recognition of opportunity; it strengthens the will

11

and reasoning powers, and teaches the cultivation and best uses of imagination, desire, the emotions and the intuitional faculty. It gives initiative, tenacity of purpose, wisdom of choice, intelligent sympathy and a thorough enjoyment of life on its higher planes.

The Master Key teaches the use of Mind Power - true Mind Power, not any of the substitutes and perversions. It has nothing to do with Hypnotism, Magic or any of the more or less fascinating deceptions by which many are led to think that something can be had for nothing.

The Master Key cultivates and develops the understanding which will enable you to control the body and thereby the health. It improves and strengthens the Memory. It develops Insight, the kind of Insight which is so rare, the kind which is the distinguishing characteristic of every successful business man, the kind which enables men to see the possibilities as well as the difficulties in every situation, the kind which enables men to discern opportunity close at hand; for thousands fail to see opportunities almost within their grasp while they are industriously working with situations which under no possibility can be made to realize any substantial return.

The Master Key develops Mental Power which means that others instinctively recognize that you are a person of force, of character - that they want to do what you want them to do. It means that you attract men and things to you; that you are what some people call "lucky"; that things "come your way"; that you have come into an understanding of the fundamental laws of Nature, and have put yourself in harmony with them; that you are in tune with Infinite; that you understand the law of attraction, the Natural laws of growth, and the Psychological laws on which all advantages in the social and business world rest.

Mental Power is creative power. It gives you the ability to create for yourself. It does not mean the ability to take something away from someone else. Nature never does things that way. Nature makes two blades of grass grow where one grew before, and Mind Power enables men to do the same thing.

The Master Key develops insight and sagacity, increased independence, the ability and disposition to be helpful. It destroys distrust, depression, fear, melancholia, and every form of lack limitation and weakness, including pain and disease. It awakens buried talents, supplies initiative, force, energy, vitality; it awakens an appreciation of the beautiful in Art, Literature and Science.

It has changed the lives of thousands of men and women, by substituting definite principles for uncertain and hazy methods - and principles for the foundation upon which every system of efficiency must rest.

Elbert Gary, the chairman of the United States Steel Corporation, said: "The services of advisors, instructors, efficiency experts in successful management are indispensable to most business enterprises of magnitude, but I deem the recognition and adoption of right principles vastly more importance." The Master Key teaches right principles, and suggests methods for making a practical application of the principles. In that, it differs from every other course of study. It teaches that the only possible value which can attach to any principle is in its application. Many read books, take home study courses, attend lectures all their lives without ever making any progress in demonstrating the value of the principles involved. The Master Key suggests methods by which the value of the principles taught may be demonstrated and put in actual practice in the daily experience.

There is a change in the thought of the world. This change is silently transpiring in our midst, and is more important than any which the world has undergone since the downfall of Paganism.

The present revolution in the opinions of all classes of men, the highest and most cultured of men as well as those of the laboring class, stands unparalleled in the history of the world.

Science has of late made such vast discoveries, has revealed such an infinity of resources, has unveiled such enormous possibilities and such unsuspected forces, that scientific men more and more hesitate to affirm certain theories as established and indubitable, or to deny certain other theories as absurd or impossible, and so a new civilization is being born. Customs, creeds, and cruelty are passing; vision, faith and service are taking their place. The fetters of tradition are being melted off from humanity, and as the dross of materialism is being consumed, thought is being liberated and truth is rising full before an astonished multitude.

The whole world is on the eve of a new consciousness; a new power and a new consciousness; a new power and a new realization of the resources within the self. The last century saw the most magnificent material progress in history. The present century will produce the greatest progress in mental and spiritual power.

Physical Science has resolved matter into molecules, molecules into atoms, atoms into energy, and it has remained for Sir Ambrose Fleming, in an address before the Royal Institution, to resolve this energy into mind. He says: "In its ultimate essence, energy may be incomprehensible by us except as an exhibition of the direct operation of that which we call Mind or Will."

Let us see what are the most powerful forces in Nature. In the mineral world everything is solid and fixed. In the animal and vegetable kingdom it is in a state of flux, forever changing, always being created and recreated. In the atmosphere we find heat, light and energy. Each realm becomes finer and more spiritual as we pass from the visible to the invisible, from the coarse to the fine, from the low potentiality to high potentiality. When we reach the invisible we find energy in its purest and most volatile state.

And as the most powerful forces of Nature are the invisible forces, so we find that the most powerful forces of man are his invisible forces, his spiritual force; and the only way in which the spiritual force can manifest is through the process of thinking. Thinking is the only activity which the spirit possesses, and thought is the only product of thinking.

Addition and subtraction are therefore spiritual transactions; reasoning is a spiritual process; ideas are spiritual conceptions; questions are spiritual searchlights and logic; argument and philosophy are spiritual machinery.

Every thought brings into action certain physical tissue, parts of the brain, nerve or muscle. This produces an actual physical change in the construction of the tissue; therefore it is only necessary to have a certain number of thoughts on a given subject in order to bring about a complete change in the physical organization of a man.

This is the process by which failure is changed to success: Thoughts of courage, power, inspiration, harmony, are substituted for thoughts of failure, despair, lack, limitation and discord, and as these thoughts take root, the physical tissue is changed and the individual sees life in a new light, old things have actually passed away, all things have become new, he is born again, this time born of the spirit; life has a new meaning for him, he is reconstructed and is filled with joy, confidence, hope, energy. He sees opportunities for success to which he was heretofore blind. He recognizes possibilities which before had no meaning for him. The thoughts of success with which he has been impregnated are radiated to those around him, and they in turn help him onward and upward. He attracts to him new and successful associates, and this in turn changes his environment; so that by this simple exercise of thought, a man changes not only himself, but his environment, circumstances and conditions.

You will see, you must see, that we are at the dawn of a new day; that the possibilities are so wonderful, so fascinating, so limitless as to be almost bewildering. A century ago, any man with an aeroplane or even a Gatling gun could have annihilated a whole army equipped with the implements of warfare then in use. So it is at present. Any man with a knowledge of the possibilities contained in the Master Key has an inconceivable advantage over the multitude.

INTRODUCTION - PART ONE

It is my privilege to enclose here Part One of The Master Key System.

Would you bring into your life more power, get the power consciousness, more health, get the health consciousness, more happiness, get the happiness consciousness. Live the spirit of these things until they become yours by right. It will then become impossible to keep them from you. The things of the world are fluid to a power within man by which he rules them.

You need not acquire this power. You already have it. But you want to understand it; you want to use it; you want to control it; you want to impregnate yourself with it, so that you can go forward and carry the world before you.

Day by day as you go on and on, as you gain momentum, as your inspiration deepens, as your plans crystallize, as you gain understanding, you will come to realize that this world is no dead pile of stones and timber, but that it is a living thing! It is made up of the beating hearts of humanity. It is a thing of life and beauty.

It is evident that it requires understanding to work with material of this description, but those who come into this understanding are inspired by a new light, a new force. They gain confidence and greater power each day. They realize their hopes and their dreams come true. Life has a deeper, fuller, clearer meaning than before.

And, now, Part One....

PART ONE

1. That much gathers more is true on every plane of existence, and that loss leads to greater loss is equally true.

2. Mind is creative, and conditions, environment and all experiences in life are the result of our habitual or predominant mental attitude.

3. The attitude of mind necessarily depends upon what we think. Therefore, the secret of all power, all achievement and all possession depends upon our method of thinking.

4. This is true because we must "be" before we can "do," and we can "do" only to the extent which we "are," and what we "are" depends upon what we "think."

5. We cannot express powers that we do not possess. The only way by which we may secure possession of power is to become conscious of power, and we can never become conscious of power until we learn that all power is from within.

6. There is a world within - a world of thought and feeling and power; of light and life and beauty; and, although invisible, its forces are mighty.

7. The world within is governed by mind. When we discover this world, we shall find the solution for every problem, the cause for every effect; and since the world within is subject to our control, all laws of power and possession are also within our control.

8. The world without is a reflection of the world within. What appears without is what has been found within. In the world within may be found infinite Wisdom, infinite Power, infinite Supply of all that is necessary, waiting for unfoldment, development and expression. If we recognize these potentialities in the world within, they will take form in the world without.

9. Harmony in the world within will be reflected in the world without by harmonious conditions, agreeable surroundings; the best of everything. It is the foundation of health and a necessary essential to all greatness, all power, all attainment, all achievement and all success.

10. Harmony in the world within means the ability to control our thoughts, and to determine for ourselves how any experience is to affect us.

11. Harmony in the world within results in optimism and affluence; affluence within results in affluence without.

12. The world without reflects the circumstances and the conditions of the consciousness within.

13. If we find wisdom in the world within, we shall have the understanding to discern the marvelous possibilities that are latent in this world within, and we shall be given the power to make these possibilities manifest in the world without.

14. As we become conscious of the wisdom in the world within, we mentally take possession of this wisdom, and by taking mental possession we come into actual possession of the power and wisdom necessary to bring into manifestation the essentials necessary for our most complete and harmonious development.

15. The world within is the practical world in which the men and women of power generate courage, hope, enthusiasm, confidence, trust and faith, by which they are given the fine intelligence to see the vision and the practical skill to make the vision real.

16. Life is an unfoldment, not an accretion. What comes to us in the world without is what we already possess in the world within.

17. All possession is based on consciousness. All gain is the result of an accumulative consciousness. All loss is the result of a scattering consciousness.

18. Mental efficiency is contingent upon harmony. Discord means confusion. Therefore, he who would acquire power must be in harmony with Natural Law.

19. We are related to the world without by the objective mind. The brain is the organ of this mind and the cerebro-spinal system of nerves puts us in conscious communication with every part of the body. This system of nerves responds to every sensation of light, heat, odor, sound and taste.

20. When this mind thinks correctly, when it understands the truth, when the thoughts sent through the cerebro-spinal nervous system to the body are constructive, these sensations are pleasant, harmonious.

21. The result is that we build strength, vitality and all constructive forces into our body, but it is through this same objective mind that all distress, sickness, lack, limitation and every form of discord and inharmony is admitted to our lives. It is therefore through the objective mind, by wrong thinking, that we are related to all destructive forces.

22. We are related to the world within by the subconscious mind. The solar plexus is the organ of this mind. The sympathetic system of nerves presides over all subjective sensations such as joy, fear, love, emotion, respiration, imagination and all other subconscious phenomena. It is through the subconscious that we are connected with the Universal Mind and brought into relation with the Infinite constructive forces of the Universe.

23. It is the coordination of these two centers of our being and the understanding of their functions which is the great secret of life. With this knowledge, we can bring the objective and subjective minds into conscious cooperation and thus coordinate the finite and the infinite. Our future is entirely within our own control; it is not at the mercy of any capricious or uncertain external power.

24. All agree that there is but one Principle or Consciousness pervading the entire Universe, occupying all space, and being essentially the same in kind at every point of its presence. It is all-powerful, all wisdom and always present. All thoughts and things are within Itself. It is all in all.

25. There is but one consciousness in the universe able to think, and when it thinks, its thoughts become objective things to it. As this Consciousness is omnipresent, it must be present within every individual; each individual must be a manifestation of that Omnipotent, Omniscient and Omnipresent Consciousness.

26. As there is only one Consciousness in the Universe that is able to think, it necessarily follows that your consciousness is identical with the Universal Consciousness, or, in other words, all mind is one mind. There is no dodging this conclusion.

27. The consciousness that focuses in your brain cells is the same consciousness which focuses in the brain cells of every other individual. Each individual is but the individualization of the Universal, the Cosmic Mind.

28. The Universal Mind is static or potential energy. It simply is. It can manifest only through the individual, and the individual can manifest only through the Universal. They are one.

29. The ability of the individual to think is his ability to act on the Universal and bring it into manifestation. Human consciousness consists only in the ability of man to think. Mind in itself is believed to be a subtle form of static energy from which arises the activities called 'thought', which is the dynamic phase of mind. Mind is static energy; thought is dynamic energy - the two phases of the same thing. Thought is therefore the vibratory force formed by converting static mind into dynamic mind.

30. As the sum of all attributes are contained in the Universal Mind, which is Omnipotent, Omniscient and Omnipresent, these attributes must be present at all times in their potential form in every individual. Therefore, when the individual thinks, the thought is compelled by its nature to embody itself in an objectivity or condition which will correspond with its origin.

31. Every thought therefore is a cause and every condition an effect; for this reason it is absolutely essential that you control your thoughts so as to bring forth only desirable conditions.

32. All power is from within, and is absolutely under your control; it comes through exact knowledge and by the voluntary exercises of exact principles.

33. It should be plain that when you acquire a thorough understanding of this law and are able to control your thought processes, you can apply it to any condition; in other words, you will have come into conscious cooperation with Omnipotent law which is the fundamental basis of all things.

34. The Universal Mind is the life principle of every atom which is in existence. Every atom is continually striving to manifest more life; all are intelligent, and all are seeking to carry out the purpose for which they were created.

35. A majority of mankind lives in the world without; few have found the world within, and yet it is the world within that makes the world without. It is therefore creative, and everything which you find in your world without has been created by you in the world within.

36. This system will bring you into a realization of power which will be yours when you understand this relation between the world without and the world within. The world within is the cause, the world without the effect; to change the effect you must change the cause.

37. You will at once see that this is a radically new and different idea. Most men try to change effects by working with effects. They fail to see that this is simply changing one form of distress for another. To remove discord, we must remove the cause, and this cause can be found only in the world within.

38. All growth is from within. This is evident in all nature. Every plant, every animal, every human is a living testimony to this great law, and the error of the ages is in looking for strength or power from without.

39. The world within is the Universal fountain of supply, and the world without is the outlet to the stream. Our ability to receive depends upon our recognition of this Universal Fountain, this Infinite Energy of which each individual is an outlet, and so is one with every other individual.

40. Recognition is a mental process. Mental action is therefore the interaction of the individual upon the Universal Mind, and as the Universal Mind is the intelligence which pervades all space and animates all living things, this mental action and reaction is the law of causation; but the principle of causation does not obtain in the individual but in the Universal Mind. It is not an objective faculty but a subjective process, and the results are seen in an infinite variety of conditions and experiences.

41. In order to express life, there must be mind. Nothing can exist without mind. Everything which exists is some manifestation of this one basic substance from which, and by which, all things have been created and are continually being recreated.

42. We live in a fathomless sea of plastic mind substance. This substance is ever alive and active. It is sensitive to the highest degree. It takes form according to the mental demand. Thought forms the mold or matrix from which the substance expresses.

43. Remember that it is in the application alone that the value consists, and that a practical understanding of this law will substitute abundance for poverty, wisdom for ignorance, harmony for discord, and freedom for tyranny, and certainly there can be no greater blessing than these from a material and social standpoint.

44. Now make the application: Select a room where you can be alone and undisturbed. Sit erect, comfortably, but do not lounge. Let your thoughts roam where they will but be perfectly still for from fifteen minutes to half an hour. Continue this for three or four days or for a week until you secure full control of your physical being.

45. Many will find this extremely difficult; others will conquer with ease, but it is absolutely essential to secure complete control of the body before you are ready to progress. Next week you will receive instructions for the next step. In the meantime, you must have mastered this one.

PART ONE - Study Questions with Answers

1. What is the world without in its relation to the world within? The world without is a reflection of the world within.

2. Upon what does all possession depend? All possession is based on consciousness.

3. How is the individual related to the objective world? The individual is related to the objective world by the objective mind; the brain is the organ of this mind.

4. How is he related to the Universal Mind? He is related to the Universal Mind by the subconscious mind; the Solar Plexus is the organ of this mind.

5. What is the Universal Mind? The Universal Mind is the life principle of every atom which is in existence.

6. How can the Individual act on the Universal? The ability of the individual to think is his ability to act upon the Universal and bring it into manifestation.

7. What is the result of this action and interaction? The result of this action and interaction is cause and effect; every thought is a cause and every condition an effect.

8. How are harmonious and desirable conditions secured? Harmonious and desirable conditions are obtained by right thinking.

9. What is the cause of all discord, disharmony, lack and limitation? Discord, disharmony, lack and limitation are the result of wrong thinking.

10. What is the source of all power? The source of all power is the world within, the Universal Fountain of Supply, the Infinite Energy of which each individual is an outlet.

INTRODUCTION - PART TWO

Our difficulties are largely due to confused ideas and ignorance of our true interests. The great task is to discover the laws of nature to which we are to adjust ourselves. Clear thinking and moral insight are, therefore, of incalculable value. All processes, even those of thought, rest on solid foundations.

The keener the sensibilities, the more acute the judgment, the more delicate the taste, the more refined the moral feelings, the more subtle the intelligence, the loftier the aspiration -- the purer and more intense are the gratifications which existence yields. Hence it is that the study of the best that has been thought in the world gives supreme pleasure.

The powers, uses and possibilities of the mind under the new interpretations are incomparably more wonderful that the most extravagant accomplishment, or even dreams of material progress. Thought is energy. Active thought is active energy. Concentrated thought is a concentrated energy. Thought concentrated on a definite purpose becomes power. This is the power which is being used by those who do not believe in the virtue of poverty, or the beauty of self-denial. They perceive that this is the talk of weaklings.

The ability to receive and manifest this power depends upon the ability to recognize the Infinite Energy ever dwelling in man, constantly creating and recreating his body and mind, and ready at any moment to manifest through him in any needful manner. In exact proportion to the recognition of this truth will be the manifestation in the outer life of the individual.

Part Two explains the method by which this is accomplished.

PART TWO

1. The operations of the mind are produced by two parallel modes of activity, the one conscious, and the other subconscious. Professor Davidson says: "He who thinks to illuminate the whole range of mental action by the light of his own consciousness is not unlike the one who should go about to illuminate the universe with a rushlight.

2. The subconscious' logical processes are carried on with a certainty and regularity which would be impossible if there existed the possibility of error. Our mind is so designed that it prepares for us the most important foundations of cognition, whilst we have not the slightest apprehension of the modus operandi.

3. The subconscious soul, like a benevolent stranger, works and makes provision for our benefit, pouring only the mature fruit into our lap; thus ultimate analysis of thought processes shows that the subconscious is the theatre of the most important mental phenomena.

4. It is through the subconscious that Shakespeare must have perceived, without effort, great truths which are hidden from the conscious mind of the student; that Phidias fashioned marble and bronze; that Raphael painted Madonna and Beethoven composed symphonies.

5. Ease and perfection depend entirely upon the degree in which we cease to depend upon the consciousness. Playing the piano, skating, operating the typewriter, the skilled trades, depend for their perfect execution on the process of the subconscious mind. The marvel of playing a brilliant piece on the piano while at the same time conducting a vigorous conversation, shows the greatness of our subconscious powers.

6. We are all aware how dependent we are upon the subconscious, and the greater, the nobler, the more brilliant our thoughts are, the more it is obvious to ourselves that the origin lies beyond our ken. We find ourselves endowed with tact, instinct, sense of the beautiful in art, music, etc., of whose origin or dwelling place we are wholly unconscious.

7. The value of the subconscious is enormous. It inspires us; it warns us; it furnishes us with names, facts and scenes from the storehouse of memory. It directs our thoughts and tastes, and accomplishes tasks so intricate that no conscious mind, even if it had the power, has the capacity for.

8. We can walk at will; we can raise the arm whenever we choose to do so, we can give our attention through eye or ear to any subject at pleasure. On the other hand, we cannot stop our heartbeats, nor the circulation of the blood, nor the growth of stature, nor the formation of nerve and muscle tissue, nor the building of the bones, nor many other important vital processes.

9. If we compare these two sets of action, the one decreed by the will of the moment, and the other proceeding in majestic, rhythmic course, subject to no vascillation but

22

constant at every moment, we stand in awe of the latter and ask to have the mystery explained. We see at once that these are the vital processes of our physical life, and we cannot avoid the inference that these all-important functions are designedly withdrawn from the domain of our outward will with its variations and transitions, and placed under the direction of a permanent and dependable power within us.

10. Of these two powers, the outward and changeable has been termed the "Conscious Mind", or the "Objective Mind" (dealing with outward objects). The interior power is called the "Subconscious Mind", or the "Subjective Mind", and besides its work on the mental plane, it controls the regular functions which make physical life possible.

11. It is necessary to have a clear understanding of their respective functions on the mental plane as well as of certain other basic principles. Perceiving and operating through the five physical senses, the conscious mind deals with the impressions and objects of the outward life.

12. It has the faculty of discrimination, carrying with it the responsibility of choice. It has the power of reasoning--whether inductive, deductive, analytical or syllogistic--and this power may be developed to a high degree. It is the seat of the will with all the energies that flow therefrom.

13. Not only can it impress other minds, but it can direct the subconscious mind. In this way the conscious mind becomes the responsible ruler and guardian of the subconscious mind. It is this high function which can completely reverse conditions in your life.

14. It is often true that conditions of fear, worry, poverty, disease, inharmony and evils of all kinds dominate us by reason of false suggestions accepted by the unguarded subconscious mind. All this the trained conscious mind can entirely prevent by its vigilant protective action. It may properly be called "the watchman at the gate" of the great subconscious domain.

15. One writer has expressed the chief distinction between the two phases of mind thus: "Conscious mind is reasoning will. Subconscious mind is instinctive desire, the result of past reasoning will."

16. The subconscious mind draws just and accurate inferences from premises furnished from outside sources. Where the premise is true, the subconscious mind reaches a faultless conclusion, but, where the premise or suggestion is an error, the whole structure falls. The subconscious mind does not engage in the process of proving. It relies upon the conscious mind, "the watchman at the gate," to guard it from mistaken impressions.

17. Receiving any suggestions as true, the subconscious mind at once proceeds to act thereon in the whole domain of its tremendous field of work. The conscious mind can suggest either truth or error; if the latter, it is at the cost of wide-reaching peril to the whole being.

18. The conscious mind ought to be on duty during every waking hour. When the "watchman" is "off guard," or when its calm judgment is suspended under a variety of circumstances, then the subconscious mind is unguarded and left open to suggestion from all sources. During the wild excitement of panic, or during the height of anger, or the impulses of the irresponsible mob, or at any other time of unrestrained passion, the conditions are most dangerous. The subconscious mind is then open to the suggestion of fear, hatred, selfishness, greed, self-depreciation and other negative forces, derived from surrounding persons or circumstances. The result is usually unwholesome in the extreme, with effects that may endure to distress it for a long time. Hence, the great importance of guarding the subconscious mind from false impressions.

19. The subconscious mind perceives by intuition. Hence, its processes are rapid. It does not wait for the slow methods of conscious reasoning. In fact, it cannot employ them.

20. The subconscious mind never sleeps, never rests, any more than does your heart, or your blood. It has been found that by plainly stating to the subconscious mind certain specific things to be accomplished, forces are set in operation that lead to the result desired. Here, then, is a source of power which places us in touch with Omnipotence. Herein is a deep principle which is well worth our most earnest study.

21. The operation of this law is interesting. Those who put it into operation find that when they go out to meet the person with whom they anticipate a difficult interview, something has been there before them and dissolved the supposed differences. Everything is changed; all is harmonious. They find that when some difficult business problem presents itself, they can afford to make delay and something suggests the proper solution; everything is properly arranged. In fact, those who have learned to trust the subconscious find that they have infinite resources at their command.

22. The subconscious mind is the seat of our principles and our aspirations. It is the fount of our artistic and altruistic ideals. These instincts can only be overthrown by an elaborate and gradual process of undermining the innate principles.

23. The subconscious mind cannot argue controversially. Hence, if it has accepted wrong suggestions, the sure method of overcoming them is by the use of a strong counter suggestion, frequently repeated, which the mind must accept, thus eventually forming new and healthy habits of thought and life, for the subconscious mind is the seat of Habit. That which we do over and over becomes mechanical; it is no longer an act of judgment, but has worn its deep grooves in the subconscious mind. This is favorable for us if the habit be wholesome and right. If it be harmful and wrong, the remedy is to recognize the omnipotence of the subconscious mind and suggest present, actual freedom. The subconscious, being creative and one with our Divine source, will at once create the freedom suggested.

24. To sum up: The normal functions of the subconscious on the physical side have to do with the regular and vital processes, with the preservation of life and the restoration of health, with the care of offspring -- which includes an instinctive desire to preserve all life and improve conditions generally.

25. On the mental side, it is the storehouse of memory; it harbors the wonderful thought messengers who work unhampered by time or space. It is the fountain of the practical initiative and constructive forces of life. It is the seat of habit.

26. On the spiritual side, it is the source of ideals, of aspiration, of the imagination, and is the channel through which we recognize our Divine Source; and in proportion as we recognize this divinity do we come into an understanding of the source of power.

27. Some one may ask: "How can the subconscious change conditions?" The reply is, because the subconscious is a part of the Universal Mind, and a part must be the same in kind and quality as the whole; the only difference is one of degree. The whole, as we know, is creative; in fact, it is the only creator there is. Consequently we find that mind is creative, and as thought is the only activity which the mind possesses, thought must necessarily be creative also.

28. But we shall find that there is a vast difference between simply thinking, and directing our thought consciously, systematically and constructively. When we do this, we place our mind in harmony with the Universal Mind. We come in tune with the Infinite; we set in operation the mightiest force in existence, the creative power of the Universal Mind. This, as everything else, is governed by natural law, and this law is the "Law of Attraction," which is that Mind is creative, and will automatically correlate with its object and bring it into manifestation.

29. Last week, I gave you an exercise for the purpose of securing control of the physical body; if you have accomplished this you are ready to advance. This time you will begin to control your thought. Always take the same room, the same chair, and the same position if possible. In some cases it is not convenient to take the same room; in this case simply make the best use of such conditions as may be available. Now be perfectly still as before, but inhibit all thought; this will give you control over all thoughts of care, worry and fear, and will enable you to entertain only the kind of thoughts you desire. Continue this exercise until you gain complete mastery.

30. You will not be able to do this for more that a few moments at a time, but the exercise is valuable because it will be a very practical demonstration of the great number of thoughts which are constantly trying to gain access to your mental world.

31. Next week you will receive instructions for an exercise which may be a little more interesting, but it is necessary that you master this one first.

"Cause and effect is as absolute and undeviating in the hidden realm of thought, as in the world of visible and material things. Mind is the master weaver, both of the interior garment of character and the outer garment of circumstance." -- James Allen.

PART TWO Study Questions with Answers

11. What are the two modes of mental activity? Conscious and subconscious.

12. Upon what do ease and perfection depend? Ease and perfection depend entirely upon the degree in which we cease to depend upon the conscious mind.

13. What is the value of the subconscious? It is enormous; it guides us, warns us, it controls the vital processes and is the seat of memory.

14. What are some of the functions of the conscious mind? It has the faculty of discrimination; it has the power of reasoning; it is the seat of the will and may impress the subconscious.

15. How has the distinction between the conscious and subconscious been expressed? "Conscious mind is reasoning will. Subconscious mind is instinctive desire, the result of past reasoning will."

16. What method is necessary in order to impress the subconscious? Mentally state what is wanted.

17. What will be the result? If the desire is in harmony with the forward movement of the great Whole, forces will be set in motion which will bring about the result.

18. What is the result of the operation of this law? Our environment reflects conditions corresponding to the predominant mental attitude which we entertain.

19. What names has been given to this law? The Law of Attraction.

20. How is the law stated? Thought is a creative energy, and will automatically correlate with is object and bring it into manifestation.

INTRODUCTION - PART THREE

You have found that the Individual may act on the Universal, and that the result of this action and interaction is cause and effect. Thought, therefore, is the cause, and the experiences with which you meet in life are the effect.

Eliminate, therefore, any possible tendency to complain of conditions as they have been, or as they are, because it rests with you to change them and make them what you would like them to be.

Direct your effort to a realization of the mental resources always at your command, from which all real and lasting power comes.

Persist in this practice until you come to a realization of the fact that there can be no failure in the accomplishment of any proper object in life, if you but understand your power and persist in your object; because the mind-forces are ever ready to lend themselves to a purposeful will, in the effort to crystallize thought and desire into actions, events and conditions.

Whereas in the beginning of each function of life and each action is the result of conscious thought, the habitual actions become automatic and the thought that controls them passes into the realm of the subconscious; yet it is just as intelligent as before. It is necessary that it become automatic, or subconscious, in order that the self-conscious mind may attend to other things. The new actions will, however, in their turn, become habitual, then automatic, then subconscious in order that the mind again may be freed from this detail and advanced to still other activities.

When you realize this, you will have found a source of power which will enable you to take care of any situation in life which may develop.

PART THREE

1. The necessary interaction of the conscious and subconscious mind requires a similar interaction between the corresponding systems of nerves. Judge Troward indicates the very beautiful method in which this interaction is effected. He says: The cerebro-spinal system is the organ of the conscious mind and the sympathetic is the organ of the subconscious. The cerebro-spinal is the channel through which we receive conscious perception from the physical senses and exercise control over the movements of the body. This system of nerves has its center in the brain.

2. The Sympathetic System has its center in a ganglionic mass at the back of the stomach known as the Solar Plexus, and is the channel of that mental action which unconsciously supports the vital functions of the body.

3. The connection between the two systems is made by the vagus nerve which passes out of the cerebral region as a portion of the voluntary system to the thorax, sending out branches to the heart and lungs; and finally, passing through the diaphragm, it loses its outer coating and becomes identified with the nerves of the Sympathetic System, so forming a connecting link between the two and making man physically a "single entity".

4. We have seen that every thought is received by the brain, which is the organ of the conscious; it is here subjected to our power of reasoning. When the objective mind has been satisfied that the thought is true, it is sent to the Solar Plexus, or the brain of the subjective mind, to be made into our flesh, to be brought forth into the world as reality. It is then no longer susceptible to any argument whatever. The subconscious mind cannot argue; it only acts. It accepts the conclusions of the objective mind as final.

5. The Solar Plexus has been likened to the sum of the body, because it is a central point of distribution for the energy which the body is constantly generating. This energy is very real energy, and this sun is a very real sun, and the energy is being distributed by very real nerves to all parts of the body, and is thrown off in an atmosphere which envelopes the body.

6. If this radiation is sufficiently strong the person is called magnetic; he is said to be filled with personal magnetism. Such a person may wield an immense power for good. His presence alone will often bring comfort to the troubled minds with which he comes in contact.

7. When the Solar Plexus is in active operation and is radiating life, energy and vitality to every part of the body, and to everyone whom he meets, the sensations are pleasant, the body is filled with health and all with whom he comes in contact experience a pleasant sensation.

8. If there is any interruption of this radiation the sensations are unpleasant, the flow of life and energy to some part of the body is stopped, and this is the cause of every ill to the human race, physical, mental or environmental.

9. Physical because the sun of the body is no longer generating sufficient energy to vitalize some part of the body; mental because the conscious mind is dependent upon the subconscious mind for the vitality necessary to support its thought; and environmental because the connection between the subconscious mind and the Universal mind is being interrupted.

10. The Solar Plexus is the point at which the part meets with the whole, where the finite becomes Infinite, where the Uncreate becomes create, the Universal becomes individualized, the Invisible becomes visible. It is the point at which life appears and there is no limit to the amount of life an individual may generate from this Solar center.

11. This center of energy is Omnipotent because it is the point of contact with all life and all intelligence. It can therefore accomplish whatever it is directed to accomplish, and herein lies the power of the conscious mind: the subconscious can and will carry out such plans and ideas as may be suggested to it by the conscious mind.

12. Conscious thought, then, is master of this sun center from which the life and energy of the entire body flows, and the quality of the thought which we entertain determines the quality of the thought which this sun will radiate, and the character of the thought which our conscious mind entertains will determine the character of the thought which this sun will radiate, and the nature of the thought which our conscious mind entertains will determine the nature of thought which this sun will radiate, and consequently will determine the nature of the experience which will result.

13. It is evident, therefore, that all we have to do is let our light shine; the more energy we can radiate, the more rapidly shall we be enabled to transmute undesirable conditions into sources of pleasure and profit. The important question, then, is how to let this light shine, how to generate this energy.

14. Non-resistant thought expands the Solar Plexus; resistant thought contracts it. Pleasant thought expands it; unpleasant thought contracts it. Thoughts of courage, power, confidence and hope all produce a corresponding state, but the one archenemy of the Solar Plexus which must be absolutely destroyed before there is any possibility of letting any light shine is fear. This enemy must be completely destroyed; he must be eliminated; he must be expelled forever; he is the cloud which hides the sun, which causes a perpetual gloom.

15. It is this personal devil which makes men fear the past, the present and the future; fear themselves, their friends and their enemies; fear everything and everybody. When fear is effectually and completely destroyed, your light will shine, the clouds will disperse and you will have found the source of power, energy and life.

16. When you find that you are really one with the Infinite power, and when you can consciously realize this power by a practical demonstration of your ability to overcome any adverse condition by the power of your thought, you will have nothing to fear. Fear will have been destroyed and you will have come into possession of your birthright.

17. It is our attitude of mind toward life which determines the experiences with which we are to meet. If we expect nothing, we shall have nothing; if we demand much, we shall receive the greater portion. The world is harsh only as we fail to assert ourselves. The criticism of the world is bitter only to those who cannot compel room for their ideas. It is fear of this criticism that causes many ideas to fail to see the light of day.

18. But the man who knows that he has a Solar Plexus will not fear criticism or anything else. He will be too busy radiating courage, confidence, and power; he will anticipate success by his mental attitude; he will pound barriers to pieces, and leap over the chasm of doubt and hesitation which fear places in his path.

19. A knowledge of our ability to consciously radiate health, strength and harmony will bring us into a realization that there is nothing to fear because we are in touch with Infinite Strength.

20. This knowledge can be gained only by making practical application of this information. We learn by doing; through practice the athlete comes powerful.

21. As the following statement is of considerable importance, I will put it in several ways, so that you cannot fail to get the full significance of it. If you are religiously inclined, I would say, you can let your light shine. If your mind has a bias toward physical science, I would say you can wake the Solar Plexus. Or, if you prefer the strictly scientific interpretation, I will say that you can impress your subconscious mind.

22. I have already told you what the result of this impression will be. It is the method in which you are now interested. You have already learned that the subconscious is intelligent and that it is creative and responsive to the will of the conscious mind. What, then, is the most natural way of making the desired impression? Mentally concentrate on the object of your desire; when you are concentrating, you are impressing the subconscious.

23. This is not the only way, but it is a simple and effective way, and the most direct way, and consequently the way in which the best results are secured. It is the method which is producing such extraordinary results that many think that miracles are being accomplished.

24. It is the method by which every great inventor, every great financier, every great statesman has been enabled to convert the subtle and invisible force of desire, faith and confidence into actual, tangible, concrete facts in the objective world.

25. The subconscious mind is a part of the Universal mind. The Universal is the creative principle of the Universe. A part must be the same in kind and quality as the whole. This means that this creative power is absolutely unlimited; it is not bound by precedent of any kind, and consequently has no prior existing pattern by which to apply its constructive principle.

26. We have found that the subconscious mind is responsive to our conscious will, which means that the unlimited creative power of the Universal Mind is within control of the conscious mind of the individual.

27. When making a practical application of this principle in accordance with the exercises given in the subsequent lessons, it is well to remember that it is not necessary to outline the method by which the subconscious will produce the results you desire. The finite cannot inform the Infinite. You are simply to say what you desire, not how you are to obtain it.

28. You are the channel by which the undifferentiated is being differentiated, and this differentiation is being accomplished by appropriation. It only requires recognition to set causes in motion which will bring about results in accordance with your desire, and this is accomplished because the Universal can act only through the individual, and the individual can act only through the Universal; they are one.

29. For your exercise this week, I will ask you to go one step further. I want you to not only be perfectly still and inhibit all thought as far as possible, but relax, let go, let the muscles take their normal condition; this will remove all pressure from the nerves, and eliminate that tension which so frequently produces physical exhaustion.

30. Physical relaxation is a voluntary exercise of the will and the exercise will be found to be of great value, as it enables the blood to circulate freely to and from the brain and body.

31. Tensions leads to mental unrest and abnormal mental activity of the mind; it produces worry, care, fear and anxiety. Relaxation is therefore an absolute necessity in order to allow the mental faculties to exercise the greatest freedom.

32. Make this exercise as thorough and complete as possible. Mentally determine that you will relax every muscle and nerve, until you feel quiet and restful and at peace with yourself and the world.

33. The Solar Plexus will then be ready to function and you will be surprised at the result.

PART THREE Study Questions with Answers

21. What system of nerves is the organ of the Conscious Mind? The Cerebro-spinal.

22. What system of nerves is the organ of the subconscious mind? The sympathetic.

23. What is the central point of distribution for energy which the body is constantly generating? The solar plexus.

24. How may this distribution be interrupted? By resistant, critical, discordant thoughts, but especially fear.

25. What is the result of such interruption? Every ill with which the human race is afflicted.

26. How may this energy be controlled and directed? By conscious thought.

27. How may fear be completely eliminated? By an understanding and recognition of the true source of all power.

28. What determines the experiences with which we meet in life? Our predominant mental attitude.

29. How may we awake the solar plexus? Mentally concentrate upon the condition which we desire to see manifested in our lives.

30. What is the creative principle of the Universe? The Universal Mind.

INTRODUCTION - PART FOUR

Enclosed herewith I hand you Part Four. This part will show you why what you think, or do, or feel is an indication of what you are.

Thought is energy and energy is power, and it is because all the religions, sciences and philosophies with which the world has heretofore been familiar have been based upon the manifestation of this energy instead of the energy itself, that the world has been limited to effects, while causes have been ignored or misunderstood.

For this reason we have God and the Devil in religion, positive and negative in science, and good and bad in philosophy.

The master key reverses the process. It is interested only in cause, and the letters received from students tell a marvelous story; they indicate conclusively that students are finding the cause whereby they may secure for themselves health, harmony, abundance, and whatever else may be necessary for their welfare and happiness.

Life is expressive and it is our business to express ourselves harmoniously and constructively. Sorrow, misery, unhappiness, disease and poverty are not necessities and we are constantly eliminating them.

But this process of eliminating consists in rising above and beyond limitation of any kind. He who has strengthened and purified his thought need not concern himself about microbes, and he who has come into an understanding of the law of abundance will go at once to the source of supply. It is thus that fate, fortune, and destiny will be controlled as readily as a captain controls his ship, or an engineer his train.

PART FOUR

1. The "I" of you is not the physical body; that is simply an instrument which the "I" uses to carry out its purposes. The "I" cannot be the Mind, for the mind is simply another instrument which the "I" uses with which to think, reason, and plan.

2. The "I" must be something which controls and directs both the body and the mind, something which determines what they shall do and how they shall act. When you come into a realization of the true nature of this "I", you will enjoy a sense of power which you have never before known.

3. Your personality is made up of countless individual characteristics, peculiarities, habits, and traits of character. These are the result of your former method of thinking, but they have nothing to do with the real "I."

4. When you say "I think" the "I" tells the mind what it shall think; when you say "I go" the "I" tells the physical body where it shall go; the real nature of this "I" is spiritual, and is the source of the real power which comes to men and women when they come into a realization of their true nature.

5. The greatest and most marvelous power which this "I" has been given is the power to think, but few people know how to think constructively, or correctly; consequently, they achieve only indifferent results. Most people allow their thoughts to dwell on selfish purposes, the inevitable result of an infantile mind. When a mind becomes mature, it understands that the germ of defeat is in every selfish thought.

6. The trained mind knows that every transaction must benefit every person who is in any way connected with the transaction, and any attempt to profit by the weakness, ignorance or necessity of another will inevitably operate to his disadvantage.

7. This is because the individual is a part of the Universal. A part cannot antagonize any other part, but, on the contrary, the welfare of each part depends upon a recognition of the interest of the whole.

8. Those who recognize this principle have a great advantage in the affairs of life. They do not wear themselves out. They can eliminate vagrant thoughts with facility. They can readily concentrate to the highest possible degree on any subject. They do not waste time or money upon objects which can be of no possible benefit to them.

9. If you cannot do these things it is because you have thus far not made the necessary effort. Now is the time to make the effort. The result will be exactly in proportion to the effort expended. One of the strongest affirmations which you can use for the purpose of strengthening the will and realizing your power to accomplish, is, "I can be what I will to be."

10. Every time you repeat it, realize who and what this "I" is; try to come into a thorough understanding of the true nature of the "I". If you do, you will become invincible -- that is, provided that your objects and purposes are constructive and are therefore in harmony with the creative principle of the Universe.

11. If you make use of this affirmation -- use it continuously, night and morning, and as often during the day as you think of it, and continue to do so until it becomes a part of you. Form the habit.

12. Unless you do this, you had better not start at all, because modern psychology tells us that when we start something and do not complete it, or make a resolution and do not keep it, we are forming the habit of failure; absolute, ignominious failure. If you do not intend to do a thing, do not start; if you do start, see it through even if the heavens fall. If you make up your mind to do something, do it; let nothing, no one, interfere. The "I" in you has determined, the thing is settled; the die is cast, there is no longer any argument.

13. If you carry out this idea, beginning with small things which you know you can control and gradually increase the effort, but never under any circumstances allowing your "I" to be overruled, you will find that you can eventually control yourself, and many men and women have found to their sorrow that it is easier to control a kingdom that to control themselves.

14. But when you have learned to control yourself you will have found the "World Within" which controls the world without; you will have become irresistible. Men and things will respond to your every wish without any apparent effort on your part.

15. This is not so strange or impossible as it may appear when you remember that the "World Within" is controlled by the "I" and that this "I" is a part or one with the Infinite "I" which is the Universal Energy or Spirit, usually called God.

16. This is not a mere statement or theory made for the purpose of confirming or establishing an idea, but it is a fact which has been accepted by the best religious thought as well as the best scientific thought.

17. Herbert Spender said: "Amid all the mysteries by which we are surrounded, nothing is more certain than that we are ever in the presence of an Infinite and Eternal Energy from which all things proceed."

18. Lyman Abbott, in an address delivered before the Alumni of Bangor Theological Seminary, said: "We are coming to think of God as dwelling in man rather than as operating on men from without."

19. Science goes a little way in its search, and stops. Science finds the ever-present Eternal Energy, but Religion finds the Power behind this energy and locates it within man. But this is by no means a new discovery. The Bible says exactly the same thing, and the language is just as plain and convincing: "Know ye not that ye are the temple of the living God?" Here, then, is the secret of the wonderful creative power of the "World Within."

20. Here is the secret of power, of mastery. To overcome does not mean to go without things. Self-denial is not success. We cannot give unless we get; we cannot be helpful unless we are strong. The Infinite is not bankrupt and we who are the representatives of

Infinite power should not be bankrupt either; and if we wish to be of service to others, we must have power and more power, but to get it we must give it, we must be of service.

21. The more we give the more we shall get; we must become a channel whereby the Universal can express activity. The Universal is constantly seeking to express itself, to be of service, and it seeks the channel whereby it can find the greatest activity, where it can do the most good, where it can be of greatest service to mankind.

22. The Universal cannot express through you as long as you are busy with your plans, your own purposes. Quiet the senses, seek inspiration, focus the mental activity on the within, dwell in the consciousness of your unity with Omnipotence. "Still water runs deep". Contemplate the multitudinous opportunities to which you have spiritual access by the Omnipresence of power.

23. Visualize the events, circumstances and conditions which these spiritual connections may assist in manifesting. Realize the fact that the essence and soul of all things is spiritual and that the spiritual is the real, because it is the life of all there is. When the spirit is gone, the life is gone; it is dead, it has ceased to exist.

24. These mental activities pertain to the world within, to the world of cause, and conditions and circumstances which result are the effect. It is thus that you become a creator. This is important work, and the higher, loftier, grander and more noble ideals which you can conceive, the more important the work will become.

25. Over-work or over-play or over-bodily activity of any kind produces conditions of mental apathy and stagnation which makes it impossible to do the more important work which results in a realization of conscious power. We should, therefore, seek the Silence frequently. Power comes through repose; it is in the Silence that we can be still, and when we are still, we can think, and thought is the secret of all attainment.

26. Thought is a mode of motion and is carried by the law of vibration the same as light or electricity. It is given vitality by the emotions through the law of love. It takes form and expression by the law of growth. It is a product of the spiritual "I", hence its Divine, spiritual, and creative nature.

27. From this it is evident that in order to express power, abundance or any other constructive purpose, the emotions must be called upon to give feeling to the thought so that it will take form. How may this purpose be accomplished? This is the vital point: How may we develop the faith, the courage, the feeling, which will result in accomplishment?

28. The reply is: By exercise. Mental strength is secured in exactly the same way that physical strength is secured, by exercise. We think something, perhaps with difficulty the first time; we think the same thing again, and it becomes easier this time; we think it again and again, it then becomes a mental habit. We continue to think the same thing. Finally it becomes automatic, we can no longer help thinking this thing. We are now positive of what we think, there is no longer any doubt about it. We are sure, we know.

29. Last week I asked you to relax, to let go physically. This week, I am going to ask you to let go mentally. If you practiced the exercise given you last week fifteen or twenty minutes a day in accordance with the instructions, you can no doubt relax physically; and anyone who cannot consciously do this quickly and completely is not a master of himself. He has not obtained freedom; he is still a slave to conditions. But I shall assume that you have mastered the exercise and are ready to take the next step, which is mental freedom.

30. This week, after taking your usual position, remove all tension by completely relaxing, then mentally let go of all adverse conditions, such as hatred, anger, worry, jealousy, envy, sorrow, trouble or disappointment of any kind.

31. You may say that you cannot "let go" of these things, but you can. You can do so by mentally determining to do so, by voluntary intention and persistence.

32. The reason that some cannot do this is because they allow themselves to be controlled by the emotions instead of by their intellect. But those who will be guided by the intellect will gain the victory. You will not succeed the first time you try, but practice makes perfect, in this as in everything else, and you must succeed in dismissing, eliminating and completely destroying these negative and destructive thoughts, because they are the seed which is constantly germinating into discordant conditions of every conceivable kind and description.

"There is nothing truer than that the quality of thought which we entertain correlates certain externals in the outside world. This is the Law from which there is no escape. And it is this Law, this correlative of the thought with its object, that from time immemorial has led the people to believe in special providence." - Wilmans

PART FOUR Study Questions with Answers

31. What is thought? Thought is spiritual energy.

32. How is it carried? By the law of vibration.

33. How is it given vitality? By the law of love.

34. How does it take form? By the law of growth.

35. What is the secret of its creative power? It is a spiritual activity.

36. How may we develop the faith, courage, and enthusiasm which will result in accomplishment? By a recognition of our spiritual nature.

37. What is the secret of Power? Service.

38. Why is this so? Because we get what we give.

39. What is the Silence? A physical stillness.

40. Of what value is it? It is the first step to self-control, self-mastery.

INTRODUCTION - PART FIVE

Enclosed herewith you will find Part Five. After studying this part carefully, you will see that every conceivable force or object or fact is the result of mind in action.

Mind in action is thought, and thought is creative. Men are thinking now as they never thought before. Therefore, this is a creative age, and the world is awarding its richest prizes to the thinkers.

Matter is powerless, passive, inert. Mind is force, energy, power. Mind shapes and controls matter. Every form which matter takes is but the expression of some pre-existing thought.

But thought works no magic transformations. It obeys natural laws; it sets in motion natural forces; it releases natural energies; it manifests in your conduct and actions, and these in turn react upon your friends and acquaintances, and eventually upon the whole of your environment.

You can originate thought, and since thoughts are creative, you can create for yourself the things you desire.

PART FIVE

1. At least ninety per cent of our mental life is subconscious, so that those who fail to make use of this mental power live within very narrow limits.

2. The subconscious can and will solve any problem for us if we know how to direct it. The subconscious processes are always at work. The only question is: are we to be simply passive recipients of this activity, or are we to consciously direct the work? Shall we have a vision of the destination to be reached, the dangers to be avoided, or shall we simply drift?

3. We have found that mind pervades every part of the physical body and is always capable of being directed or impressed by authority coming from the objective or the more dominant portion of the mind.

4. The mind, which pervades the body, is largely the result of heredity, which, in turn, is simply the result of all the environments of all past generations on the responsive and ever-moving life forces. An understanding of this fact will enable us to use our authority when we find some undesirable trait of character manifesting.

5. We can consciously use all the desirable characteristics with which we have been provided and we can repress and refuse to allow the undesirable ones to manifest.

6. Again, this mind, which pervades our physical body, is not only the result of hereditary tendencies, but is the result of home, business and social environment, where countless thousands of impressions, ideas, prejudices and similar thoughts have been received. Much of this has been received from others, the result of opinions, suggestions or statements; much of it is the result of our own thinking, but nearly all of it has been accepted with little or no examination or consideration.

8. The idea seemed plausible, the conscious received it, passed it on to the subconscious, where it was taken up by the Sympathetic System and passed on to be built into our physical body. "The word has become flesh."

9. This, then, is the way we are consistently creating and recreating ourselves. We are today the result of our past thinking, and we shall be what we are thinking today. The Law of Attraction is bringing to us not the things we should like, or the things we wish for, or the things someone else has, but it brings us "our own," the things which we have created by our thought processes, whether consciously or unconsciously. Unfortunately, many of us are creating these things unconsciously.

10. If either of us were building a home for ourselves, how careful we would be in regard to the plans. How we should study every detail, how we should watch the material and select only the best of everything; and yet how careless we are when it comes to building our Mental Home, which is infinitely more important than any physical home, as everything which can possibly enter into our lives depends upon the character of the material which enters into the construction of our Mental Home.

11. What is the character of this material? We have seen that it is the result of the impressions which we have accumulated in the past and stored away in our subconscious Mentality. If these impressions have been of fear, of worry, of care, of anxiety; if they have been despondent, negative, doubtful -- then the texture of the material which we are weaving today will be of the same negative material. Instead of being of any value, it will be mildewed and rotten and will bring us only more toil and care and anxiety. We shall be forever busy trying to patch it up and make it appear at least genteel.

12. But if we have stored away nothing but courageous thought, if we have been optimistic, positive, and have immediately thrown any kind of negative thought on the scrap pile, have refused to have anything to do with it, have refused to associate with it or become identified with it in any way, what then is the result? Our mental material is now of the best kind. We can weave any kind of material we want, we can use any color we wish. We know that the texture is firm, that the material is solid, that it will not fade; and we have no fear, no anxiety concerning the future. There is nothing to cover, there are no patches to hide.

13. These are psychological facts. There is no theory or guesswork about these thinking processes; there is nothing secret about them; in fact, they are so plain that every one can understand them. The thing to do is to have a mental housecleaning, and to have this housecleaning every day, and keep the house clean. Mental, moral and physical cleanliness are absolutely indispensable if we are to make progress of any kind.

14. When this mental housecleaning process has been completed, the material which is left will be suitable for the making of the kind of ideals or mental images which we desire to realize.

15. There is a fine estate awaiting a claimant. Its broad acres, with abundant crops, running water and fine timber, stretch away as far as the eye can see. There is a mansion, spacious and cheerful, with rare pictures, a well-stocked library, rich hangings, and every comfort and luxury. All the heir has to do is to assert his heirship, take possession, and use the property. He must use it; he must not let it decay, for use is the condition on which he holds it. To neglect it is to lose possession.

16. In the domain of mind and spirit, in the domain of practical power, such an estate is yours. You are the heir! You can assert your heirship, and possess and use this rich inheritance. Power over circumstances is one of its fruits; health, harmony and prosperity are assets upon its balance sheet. It offers you poise and peace. It costs you only the labor of studying and harvesting its great resources. It demands no sacrifice, except the loss of your limitations, your servitudes, your weakness. It clothes you with self-honor, and puts a scepter in your hands.

17. To gain this estate, three processes are necessary: You must earnestly desire it. You must assert your claim. You must take possession.

18. You admit that those are not burdensome conditions.

19. You are familiar with the subject of heredity. Darwin, Huxley, Haeckel, and other physical scientists have piled evidence mountain-high that heredity is a law attending progressive creation. It is progressive heredity which gives man his erect attitude, his power of motion, the organs of digestions, blood circulation, nerve force, muscular force, bone structure and a host of other faculties on the physical side. There are even more impressive facts concerning heredity of mind force. All these constitute what may be called your human heredity.

20. But there is a heredity which the physical scientists have not compassed. It lies beneath and antecedent to all their researches. At a point where they throw up their hands in despair, saying they cannot account for what they see, this Divine heredity is found in full sway.

21. It is the benignant force which decrees primal creation. It thrills down from the Divine, direct into every created being. It originates life, which the physical scientist has not done, nor ever can do. It stands out among all forces supreme, unapproachable. No human heredity can approach it. No human heredity measures up to it.

22. This Infinite Life flows through you, is you. Its doorways are but the faculties which comprise your consciousness. To keep open these doors is the Secret of Power. Is it not worthwhile to make the effort?

23. The great fact is that the source of all life and all power is from within. Persons, circumstances and events may suggest need and opportunities, but the insight, strength and power to answer these needs will be found within.

24. Avoid counterfeits. Build firm foundations for your consciousness upon forces which flow direct from the Infinite source, the Universal Mind of which you are the image and likeness.

25. Those who have come into possession of this inheritance are never quite the same again. They have come into possession of a sense of power hitherto undreamed of. They can never again be timid, weak, vacillating, or fearful. They are indissolubly connected with Omnipotence. Something in them has been aroused; they have suddenly discovered that they possess a tremendous latent ability of which they were heretofore entirely unconscious.

26. This power is from within, but we cannot receive it unless we give it. Use is the condition upon which we hold this inheritance. We are each of us but the channel through which the Omnipotent power is being differentiated into form. Unless we give, the channel is obstructed and we can receive no more. This is true on every plane of existence and in every field of endeavor and all walks of life. The more we give, the more we get. The athlete who wishes to get strong must make use of the strength he has, and the more he gives the more he will get. The financier who wishes to make money must make use of the money he has, for only by using it can he get more.

27. The merchant who does not keep his goods going out will soon have none coming in. The corporation which fails to give efficient service will soon lack customers. The attorney who fails to get results will soon lack clients, and so it goes everywhere. Power is contingent upon a proper use of the power already in our possession. What is true in every field of endeavor, every experience in life, is true of the power from which every other power known among men is begotten -- spiritual power. Take away the spirit and what is left? Nothing.

28. If then the spirit is all there is, upon the recognition of this fact must depend the ability to demonstrate all power, whether physical, mental or spiritual.

29. All possession is the result of the accumulative attitude of mind, or the money consciousness. This is the magic wand which will enable you to receive the idea, and it will formulate plans for you to execute, and you will find as much pleasure in the execution as in the satisfaction of attainment and achievement.

30. Now, go to your room, take the same seat, the same position as heretofore, and mentally select a place which has pleasant associations. Make a complete mental picture of it: See the buildings, the grounds, the trees, friends, associations, everything complete. At first, you will find yourself thinking of everything under the sun, except the ideal upon which you desire to concentrate. But do not let that discourage you. Persistence will win, but persistence requires that you practice these exercises every day without fail.

PART FIVE Study Questions with Answers

41. What proportion of our mental life is subconscious? At least ninety per cent.

42. Is this vast mental storehouse generally utilized? No.

43. Why not? Few understand or appreciate the fact that it is an activity which they may consciously direct.

44. Where has the conscious mind received its governing tendencies? From heredity -- which means that it is the result of all the environments of all past generations.

45. What is the law of attraction bringing to us? Our "Own."

46. What is our "Own"? What we inherently are, and is the result of our past thinking, both conscious and subconscious.

47. Of what is the material with which we construct our mental home composed? The thoughts which we entertain.

48. What is the Secret of Power? A recognition of the omnipresence of omnipotence.

49. Where does it originate? All life and all power is from within.

50. Upon what is the possession of power contingent? Upon a proper use of the power already in our possession.

INTRODUCTION - PART SIX

It is my privilege to enclose Part Six. This part will give you an excellent understanding of the most wonderful piece of mechanism which has ever been created. A mechanism whereby you may create for yourself Health, Strength, Success, Prosperity or any other condition which you desire. Necessities are demands, and demands create action, and actions bring about results. The process of evolution is constantly building our tomorrows out of our todays. Individual development, like Universal development, must be gradual with an ever-increasing capacity and volume.

The knowledge that if we infringe upon the rights of others, we become moral thorns and find ourselves entangled at every turn of the road, should be an indication that success is contingent upon the highest moral ideal, which is "The greatest good to the greatest number."

Aspiration, desire and harmonious relations constantly and persistently maintained will accomplish results. The greatest hindrance is erroneous and fixed ideas.

To be in tune with eternal truth we must possess poise and harmony within. In order to receive intelligence the receiver must be in tune with the transmitter.

Thought is a product of Mind and Mind is creative, but this does not mean that the Universal will change its modus operandi to suit us or our ideas, but it does mean that we can come into harmonious relationship with the Universal, and when we have accomplished this we may ask anything to which we are entitled, and the way will be made plain.

PART SIX

1. The Universal Mind is so wonderful that it is difficult to understand its utilitarian powers and possibilities and its unlimited producing effects.

2. We have found that this Mind is not only all intelligence, but all substance. How, then, is it to be differentiated in form? How are we to secure the effect which we desire?

3. Ask any electrician what the effect of electricity will be and he will reply that "Electricity is a form of motion and its effect will depend upon the mechanism to which it is attached." Upon this mechanism will depend whether we shall have heat, light, power, music or any of the other marvelous demonstration of power to which this vital energy has been harnessed.

4. What effect can be produced by thought? The reply is that thought is mind in motion (just as wind is air in motion), and its effect will depend entirely on the "mechanism to which it is attached."

5. Here, then, is the secret of all mental power; it depends entirely on the mechanism which we attach.

6. What is this mechanism? You know something of the mechanism which has been invented by Edison, Bell, Marconi and other electrical wizards, by which place and space and time have become only figures of speech, but did you ever stop to think that the mechanism which has been given you for transforming the Universal, Omnipresent Potential Power was invented by a greater inventor than Edison?

7. We are accustomed to examining the mechanism of the implements which we use for tilling the soil, and we try to get an understanding of the mechanism of the automobile which we drive, but most of us are content to remain in absolute ignorance of the greatest piece of mechanism which as ever come into existence: the brain of man.

8. Let us examine the wonders of this mechanism; perhaps we shall thereby get a better understanding of the various effects of which it is the cause.

9. In the first place, there is the great mental world in which we live and move and have our being; this world is omnipotent, omniscient and omnipresent. It will respond to our desire in direct ratio to our purpose and faith. The purpose must be in accordance with the law of our being; that is, it must be creative or constructive. Our faith must be strong enough to generate a current of sufficient strength to bring our purpose into manifestation. "As thy faith is, so be it unto thee," bears the stamp of scientific test.

10. The effects which are produced in the world without are the result of the action and reaction of the individual upon the universal; that is the process which we call thinking. The brain is the organ through which this process is accomplished. Think of the wonder of it all! Do you love music, flowers, literature, or are you inspired by the thought of ancient or modern genius? Remember, every beauty to which you respond must have its corresponding outline in your brain before you can appreciate it.

11. There is not a single virtue or principle in the storehouse of nature which the brain cannot express. The brain is an embryonic world, ready to develop at any time as necessity may arise. If you can comprehend that this is a scientific truth and one of the wonderful laws of nature, it will be easier for you to get an understanding of the mechanism by which these extraordinary results are being accomplished.

12. The nervous system has been compared to an electric circuit with its battery of cells in which force is originated, and its white matter to insulated wires by which the current is conveyed; it is through these channels that every impulse or desire is carried through the mechanism.

13. The spinal cord is the great motor and sensory pathway by which messages are conveyed to and from the brain. Then, there is the blood supply plunging through the veins and arteries, renewing our energy and strength, the perfectly arranged structure upon which the entire physical body rests. And finally, the delicate and beautiful skin clothing the entire mechanism is a mantle of beauty.

14. This then is the "Temple of the living God" and the individual "I" is given control, and upon his understanding of the mechanism which is within his control will the result depend.

15. Every thought sets the brain cells in action. At first the substance upon which the thought is directed fails to respond, but if the thought is sufficiently refined and concentrated, the substance finally yields and expresses perfectly.

16. This influence of the mind can be exerted upon any part of the body, causing the elimination of any undesirable effect.

17. A perfect conception and understanding of the laws governing in the mental world cannot fail to be of inestimable value in the transaction of business, as it develops the power of discernment and gives a clearer understanding and appreciation of facts.

18. The man who looks within instead of without cannot fail to make use of the mighty forces which will eventually determine his course in life and so bring him into vibration with all that is best, strongest and most desirable.

19. Attention or concentration is probably the most important essential in the development of mind culture. The possibilities of attention when properly directed are so startling that they would hardly appear credible to the uninitiated. The cultivation of attention is the distinguishing characteristic of every successful man or woman, and is the very highest personal accomplishment which can be acquired.

20. The power of attention can be more readily understood by comparing it with a magnifying glass in which the rays of sunlight are focused; they possess no particular strength as long as the glass is moved about and the rays directed from one place to another; but let the glass be held perfectly still and let the rays be focused on one spot for any length of time, the effect will become immediately apparent.

21. So with the power of thought: Let power be dissipated by scattering the thought from one object to another, and no result is apparent; but focus this power through attention or concentration on any single purpose for any length of time and nothing becomes impossible.

22. A very simple remedy for a very complex situation, some will say. All right, try it, you who have had no experience in concentrating the thought on a definite purpose or object. Choose any single object and concentrate your attention on it for a definite purpose for even ten minutes -- you cannot do it, the mind will wander a dozen times and it will be necessary to bring it back to the original purpose, and each time the effect will have been lost and at the end of the ten minutes nothing will have been gained, because you have not been able to hold your thought steadily to the purpose.

23. It is, however, through attention that you will finally be able to overcome obstacles of any kind that appear in your path onward and upward, and the only way to acquire this wonderful power is by practice -- practice makes perfect, in this as in anything else.

24. In order to cultivate the power of attention, bring a photograph with you to the same seat in the same room, in the same position as heretofore. Examine it closely at least ten minutes: note the expression of the eyes, the form of the features, the clothing, the way the hair is arranged; in fact, note every detail shown on the photograph carefully. Now cover it and close your eyes and try to see it mentally. If you can see every detail perfectly and can form a good mental image of the photograph, you are to be congratulated; if not, repeat the process until you can.

25. This step is simply for the purpose of preparing the soil; next week we shall be ready to sow the seed.

26. It is by such exercises as these that you will finally be able to control your mental moods, your attitude, your consciousness.

27. Great financiers are learning to withdraw from the multitude more and more, that they may have more time for planning, thinking and generating the right mental moods.

28. Successful businessmen are constantly demonstrating the fact that it pays to keep in touch with the thought of other successful businessmen.

29. A single idea may be worth millions of dollars, and these ideas can only come to those who are receptive, who are prepared to receive them, who are in successful frame of mind.

30. Men are learning to place themselves in harmony with the Universal Mind. They are learning the unity of all things. They are learning the basic methods and principles of thinking, and this is changing conditions and multiplying results.

31. They are finding that circumstances and environment follow the trend of mental and spiritual progress. They find that growth follows knowledge; action follows inspiration; opportunity follows perception; always the spiritual first, then the transformation into the infinite and illimitable possibilities of achievement.

32. As the individual is but the channel for the differentiation of the Universal, these possibilities are necessarily inexhaustible.

33. Thought is the process by which we may absorb the Spirit of Power and hold the result in our inner consciousness until it becomes a part of our ordinary consciousness. The method of accomplishing this result by the persistent practice of a few fundamental principles, as explained in this System, is the master key which unlocks the storehouse of Universal Truth.

34. The two great sources of human suffering at present are bodily disease and mental anxiety. These may be readily traced to the infringement of some Natural Law. This is, no doubt, owing to the fact that so far knowledge has largely remained partial, but the clouds of darkness which have accumulated through long ages are beginning to roll away, and with them many of the miseries that attend imperfect information.

"That a man can change himself, improve himself, re-create himself, control his environment, and master his own destiny is the conclusion of every mind who is wide-awake to the power of right thought in constructive action." - Larson

PART SIX Study Questions with Answers

51. What are some of the effects which can be produced by electricity? Heat, light, power, music.

52. Upon what do these various effects depend? Upon the mechanism to which electricity is attached.

53. What is the result of the action and interaction of the individual mind upon the Universal? The conditions and experiences with which we meet.

54. How may these conditions be changed? By changing the mechanism by which the Universal is differentiated in form.

55. What is this mechanism? The brain.

56. How may it be changed? By the process we call thinking. Thoughts produce brain cells, and these cells respond to the corresponding thought in the Universal.

57. Of what value is the power of concentration? It is the very highest personal accomplishment which can be acquired, and the distinguishing characteristic of every successful man or woman.

58. How may it be acquired? By faithfully practicing the exercises in this System.

59. Why is this so important? Because it will enable us to control our thoughts, and since thoughts are causes, conditions must be effects. If we can control the cause we can also control the effect.

60. What is changing conditions and multiplying results in the objective world? Men are learning the basic methods of constructive thinking.

INTRODUCTION - PART SEVEN

Through all the ages man has believed in an invisible power, through which and by which all things have been created and are continually being re-created.

We may personalize this power and call it God, or we may think of it as the essence or spirit which permeates all things, but in either case the effect is the same.

So far as the individual is concerned, the objective -- the physical, the visible -- is the personal, that which can be cognized by the senses. It consists of body, brain and nerves. The subjective is the spiritual, the invisible, the impersonal.

The personal is conscious because it is a personal entity. The impersonal, being the same in kind and quality as all other Being, is not conscious of itself and has therefore been termed the subconscious. The personal, or conscious, has the power of will and choice, and can therefore exercise discrimination in the selection of methods whereby to bring about the solution of difficulties. The impersonal, or spiritual, being a part or one with the source and origin of all power, can necessarily exercise no such choice, but, on the contrary, it has Infinite resources at its command. It can and does bring about results by methods concerning which the human or individual mind can have no possible conception.

You will therefore see that it is your privilege to depend upon the human will with all its limitations and misconceptions, or you may utilize the potentialities of Infinity by making use of the subconscious mind. Here, then, is the scientific explanation of the wonderful power which has been put within your control, if you but understand, appreciate and recognize it.

One method of consciously utilizing this omnipotent power is outlined in Part Seven.

PART SEVEN

1. Visualization is the process of making mental images, and the image is the mold or model which will serve as a pattern from which your future will emerge.

2. Make the pattern clear and make it beautiful. Do not be afraid; make it grand. Remember that no limitation can be placed upon you by any one but yourself. You are not limited as to cost or material. Draw on the Infinite for your supply, construct it in your imagination; it will have to be there before it will ever appear anywhere else.

3. Make the image clear and clean-cut, hold it firmly in the mind and you will gradually and constantly bring the thing nearer to you. You can be what "you will to be."

4. This is another psychological fact which is well known, but unfortunately, reading about it will not bring about any result which you may have in mind; it will not even help you to form the mental image, much less bring it into manifestation. Work is necessary - labor, hard mental labor, the kind of effort which so few are willing to put forth.

5. The first step is idealization. It is likewise the most important step, because it is the plan on which you are going to build. It must be solid; it must be permanent. The architect, when he plans a 30-story building, has every line and detail pictured in advance. The engineer, when he spans a chasm, first ascertains the strength requirements of a million separate parts.

6. They see the end before a single step is taken; so you are to picture in your mind what you want. You are sowing the seed, but before sowing any seed you want to know what the harvest is to be. This is Idealization. If you are not sure, return to the chair daily until the picture becomes plain; it will gradually unfold. First the general plan will be dim, but it will take shape, the outline will take form, then the details, and you will gradually develop the power by which you will be enabled to formulate plans which will eventually materialize in the objective world. You will come to know what the future holds for you.

7. Then comes the process of visualization. You must see the picture more and more complete, see the detail, and as the details begin to unfold, the ways and means for bringing it into manifestation will develop. One thing will lead to another. Thought will lead to action, action will develop methods, methods will develop friends, and friends will bring about circumstances, and, finally, the third step, or Materialization, will have been accomplished.

8. We all recognize the Universe must have been thought into shape before it ever could have become a material fact. And if we are willing to follow along the lines of the Great Architect of the Universe, we shall find our thoughts taking form, just as the universe took concrete form. It is the same mind operating through the individual. There is no difference in kind or quality, the only difference is one of degree.

9. The architect visualizes his building; he sees it as he wishes it to be. His thought becomes a plastic mold from which the building will eventually emerge, a high one or a low one, a beautiful one or a plain one. His vision takes form on paper and eventually the necessary material is utilized and the building stands complete.

10. The inventor visualizes his idea in exactly the same manner. For instance, Nikola Tesla, he with the giant intellect, one of the greatest inventors of all ages, the man who has brought forth the most amazing realities, always visualizes his inventions before attempting to work them out. He did not rush to embody them in form and then spend his time in correcting defects. Having first built up the idea in his imagination, he held it there as a mental picture, to be reconstructed and improved by his thought. "In this way," he writes in the Electrical Experimenter, "I am enabled to rapidly develop and perfect a conception without touching anything. When I have gone so far as to embody in the invention every possible improvement I can think of, and see no fault anywhere, I put into concrete the product of my brain. Invariably my device works as I conceived it should; in twenty years there has not been a single exception."

11. If you can conscientiously follow these directions, you will develop Faith, the kind of Faith that is the "Substance of things hoped for, the evidence of things not seen". You will develop confidence, the kind of confidence that leads to endurance and courage. You will develop the power of concentration which will enable you to exclude all thoughts except the ones which are associated with your purpose.

12. The law is that thought will manifest in form, and only one who knows how to be the divine thinker of his own thoughts can ever take a Master's place and speak with authority.

13. Clearness and accuracy are obtained only by repeatedly having the image in mind. Each repeated action renders the image more clear and accurate than the preceding, and in proportion to the clearness and accuracy of the image will the outward manifestation be. You must build it firmly and securely in your mental world, the world within, before it can take form in the world without, and you can build nothing of value, even in the mental world unless you have the proper material. When you have the material you can build anything you wish, but make sure of your material. You cannot make broadcloth from shoddy.

14. This material will be brought out by millions of silent mental workers and fashioned into the form of the image which you have in mind.

15. Think of it! You have over five million of these mental workers, ready and in active use; brain cells they are called. Besides this, there is another reserve force of at least an equal number, ready to be called into action at the slightest need. Your power to think, then, is almost unlimited, and this means that your power to create the kind of material which is necessary to build for yourself any kind of environment which you desire is practically unlimited.

16. In addition to these millions of mental workers, you have billions of mental workers in the body, every one of which is endowed with sufficient intelligence to understand

and act upon any message or suggestion given. These cells are all busy creating and recreating the body, but in addition to this, they are endowed with psychic activity whereby they can attract to themselves the substance necessary for perfect development.

17. They do this by the same law and in the same manner that every form of life attracts to itself the necessary material for growth. The oak, the rose, the lily, all require certain material for their most perfect expression and they secure it by silent demand, the Law of Attraction, the most certain way for you to secure what you require for your most complete development.

18. Make the Mental Image. Make it clear, distinct, perfect; hold it firmly. The ways and means will develop, supply will follow the demand, you will be led to do the right thing at the right time and in the right way. Earnest Desire will bring about Confident Expectation, and this in turn must be reinforced by Firm Demand. These three cannot fail to bring about Attainment, because the Earnest Desire is the feeling, the Confident Expectation is the thought, and the Firm Demand is the will, and as we have seen, feeling gives vitality to thought and the will holds it steadily until the law of Growth brings it into manifestation.

19. Is it not wonderful that man has such tremendous power within himself, such transcendental faculties concerning which he had no conception? Is it not strange that we have always been taught to look for strength and power "without?" We have been taught to look everywhere but "within" and whenever this power manifested in our lives we were told that it was something supernatural.

20. There are many who have come to an understanding of this wonderful power, and who make serious and conscientious efforts to realize health, power and other conditions, and seem to fail. They do not seem able to bring the Law into operation. The difficulty in nearly every case is that they are dealing with externals. They want money, power, health and abundance, but they fail to realize that these are effects and can come only when the cause is found.

21. Those who will give no attention to the world without will seek only to ascertain the truth, will look only for wisdom, will find that this wisdom will unfold and disclose the source of all power, that it will manifest in thought and purpose which will create the external conditions desired. This truth will find expression in noble purpose and courageous action.

22. Create ideals only. Give no thought to external conditions. Make the world within beautiful and opulent, and the world without will express and manifest the condition which you have within. You will come into a realization of your power to create ideals and these ideals will be projected into the world of effect.

23. For instance, a man is in debt. He will be continually thinking about the debt, concentrating on it, and as thoughts are causes the result is that he not only fastens the debt closer to him, but actually creates more debt. He is putting the great law of Attraction into operation with the usual and inevitable result -- Loss leads to greater

"Loss."

24. What, then, is the correct principle? Concentrate on the things you want, not on the things you do not want. Think of abundance; idealize the methods and plans for putting the Law of Abundance into operation. Visualize the condition which the Law of Abundance creates; this will result in manifestation.

25. If the law operates perfectly to bring about poverty, lack and every form of limitation for those who are continually entertaining thoughts of lack and fear, it will operate with the same certainty to bring about conditions of abundance and opulence for those who entertain thoughts of courage and power.

26. This is a difficult problem for many. We are too anxious; we manifest anxiety, fear, distress; we want to do something; we want to help; we are like a child who has just planted a seed and every fifteen minutes goes and stirs up the earth to see if it is growing. Of course, under such circumstances, the seed will never germinate, and yet this is exactly what many of us do in the mental world.

27. We must plant the seed and leave it undisturbed. This does not mean that we are to sit down and do nothing, by no means; we will do more and better work then we have ever done before, new channels will constantly be provided, new doors will open. All that is necessary is to have an open mind, be ready to act when the time comes.

28. Thought force is the most powerful means of obtaining knowledge, and if concentrated on any subject will solve the problem. Nothing is beyond the power of human comprehension, but in order to harness thought force and make it do your bidding, work is required.

29. Remember that thought is the fire that creates the steam that turns the wheel of fortune, upon which your experiences depend.

30. Ask yourself a few questions and then reverently await the response. Do you not now and then feel the self with you? Do you assert this self or do you follow the majority? Remember that majorities are always led; they never lead. It was the majority that fought, tooth and nail, against the steam engine, the power loom and every other advance or improvement ever suggested.

31. For your exercise this week, visualize your friend; see him exactly as you last saw him. See the room, the furniture, recall the conversation. Now see his face, see it distinctly. Now talk to him about some subject of mutual interest; see his expression change, watch him smile. Can you do this? All right, you can. Then arouse his interest, tell him a story of adventure; see his eyes light up with the spirit of fun or excitement. Can you do all of this? If so, your imagination is good, you are making excellent progress.

PART SEVEN Study Questions with Answers

61. What is visualization? The process of making mental pictures.

62. What is the result of this method of thought? By holding the image or picture in mind, we can gradually but surely bring the thing nearer to us. We can be what we will to be.

63. What is Idealization? It is a process of visualizing or idealizing the plans which will eventually materialize in our objective world.

64. Why are clearness and accuracy necessary? Because "seeing" creates "feeling" and "feeling" creates "being." First the mental, then the emotional, then the unlimitted possibilities of achievement.

65. How are they obtained? Each repeated action renders the image more accurate than the former one.

66. How is the material for the construction of your mental image secured? By millions of mental workers; Brain cells they are called.

67. How are the necessary conditions for bringing about the materialization of your ideal in the objective world secured? By the Law of Attraction, the natural law by which all conditions and experiences are brought about.

68. What three steps are necessary in order to bring this law into operation? Earnest Desire, Confident Expectation, Firm Demand.

69. Why do many fail? Because they concentrate on loss, disease and disaster. The law is operating perfectly; the things they fear are coming upon them.

70. What is the alternative? Concentrate on the ideals which you desire to see manifested in your life.

INTRODUCTION - PART EIGHT

In this Part you will find that you may freely choose what you think, but the result of your thought is governed by an immutable law! Is not this a wonderful thought? Is it not wonderful to know that our lives are not subject to caprice or variability of any kind, that they are governed by law? This stability is our opportunity, because by complying with the law we can secure the desired effect with invariable precision. It is the Law which makes the Universe one grand paean of Harmony. If it were not for law, the Universe would be a Chaos instead of a Cosmos.

Here, then, is the secret of the origin of both good and evil. This is all the good and evil there ever was or ever will be.

Let me illustrate. Thought results in action. If your thought is constructive and harmonious, the result will be good; if your thought is destructive or inharmonious, the result will be evil.

There is therefore but one law, one principle, one cause, one Source of Power, and good and evil are simply words which have been coined to indicate the result of our action, or our compliance or non-compliance with this law.

The importance of this is well illustrated in the lives of Emerson and Carlyle. Emerson loved the good and his life was a symphony of peace and harmony. Carlyle hated the bad, and his life was a record of perpetual discord and inharmony.

Here we have two grand men, each intent upon achieving the same ideal, but one makes use of constructive thought and is therefore in harmony with Natural Law, the other makes use of destructive thought and therefore brings upon himself discord of every kind and character.

It is evident therefore that we are to hate nothing, not even the "bad", because hatred is destructive, and we shall soon find that by entertaining destructive thought we are sowing the "wind" and in turn shall reap the "whirlwind."

PART EIGHT

1. Thought contains a vital principle, because it is the creative principle of the Universe and by its nature will combine with other similar thoughts.

2. As the one purpose of life is growth, all principles underlying existence must contribute to give it effect. Thought therefore takes form, and the law of growth eventually brings it into manifestation.

3. You may freely choose what you think, but the result of your thought is governed by an immutable law. Any line of thought persisted in cannot fail to produce its result in the character, health and circumstances of the individual. Methods whereby we can substitute habits of constructive thinking for those which we have found produce only undesirable effects are therefore of primary importance.

4. We all know that this is by no means easy. Mental habits are difficult to control, but it can be done and the way to do it is to begin at once to substitute constructive thought for destructive thought. Form the habit of analyzing every thought. If it is necessary, if its manifestation in the objective will be a benefit not only to yourself, but to all whom it may affect in any way. Keep it, treasure it; it is of value; it is in tune with the Infinite; it will grow and develop and produce fruit a hundred fold. On the other hand, it will be well for you to keep this quotation from George Matthews Adams in mind, "Learn to keep the door shut, keep out of your mind, out of your office, and out of your world, every element that seeks admittance with no definite helpful end in view."

5. If your thought has been critical or destructive, and has resulted in any condition of discord or inharmony in your environment, it may be necessary for you to cultivate a mental attitude which will be conducive to constructive thought.

6. The imagination will be found to be a great assistance in this direction; the cultivation of the imagination leads to the development of the ideal out of which your future will emerge.

7. The imagination gathers up the material by which the Mind weaves the fabric in which your future is to be clothed.

8. Imagination is the light by which we can penetrate new worlds of thought and experience.

9. Imagination is the mighty instrument by which every discoverer, every inventor, opened the way from precedent to experience. Precedent said, "It cannot be done"; experience said, "It is done."

10. Imagination is a plastic power, molding the things of sense into new forms and ideals.

11. Imagination is the constructive form of thought which must precede every constructive form of action.

12. A builder cannot build a structure of any kind until he has first received the plans

58

from the architect, and the architect must get them from his imagination.

13. The Captain of Industry cannot build a giant corporation which may coordinate hundreds of smaller corporations and thousands of employees, and utilize millions of dollars of capital until he has first created the entire work in his imagination. Objects in the material world are as clay in the potter's hand. It is in the Master Mind that the real things are created, and it is by the use of the imagination that the work is done. In order to cultivate the imagination it must be exercised. Exercise is necessary to cultivate mental muscle as well as physical muscle. It must be supplied with nourishment or it cannot grow.

14. Do not confuse Imagination with Fancy, or that form of daydreaming in which some people like to indulge. Daydreaming is a form of mental dissipation which may lead to mental disaster.

15. Constructive imagination means mental labor, by some considered to be the hardest kind of labor, but if so, it yields the greatest returns, for all the great things in life have come to men and women who had the capacity to think, to imagine, and to make their dreams come true.

16. When you have become thoroughly conscious of the fact that Mind is the only creative principle, that it is Omnipotent, Omniscient and Omnipresent, and that you can consciously come into harmony with this Omnipotence through your power of thought, you will have taken a long step in the right direction.

17. The next step is to place yourself in position to receive this power. As it is Omnipresent, it must be within you. We know that this is so because we know that all power is from within, but it must be developed, unfolded, cultivated; in order to do this we must be receptive, and this receptivity is acquired just as physical strength is gained, by exercise.

18. The law of attraction will certainly and unerringly bring to you the conditions, environment, and experiences in life corresponding with your habitual, characteristic, predominant mental attitude. Not what you think once in a while when you are in church, or have just read a good book, BUT your predominant mental attitude is what counts.

19. You cannot entertain weak, harmful, negative thoughts ten hours a day and expect to bring about beautiful, strong and harmonious conditions by ten minutes of strong, positive, creative thought.

20. Real power comes from within. All power that anybody can possibly use is within man, only waiting to be brought into visibility by his first recognizing it, and then affirming it as his, working it into his consciousness until he becomes one with it.

21. People say that they desire abundant life, and so they do, but so many interpret this to mean that if they will exercise their muscles or breathe scientifically, eat certain foods in certain ways, drink so many glasses of water every day of just a certain temperature, keep out of drafts, they will attain the abundant life they seek. The result of such methods is but indifferent. However, when man awakens to the truth, and affirms his oneness with all Life, he finds that he takes on the clear eye, the elastic step, the vigor of youth; he finds that he has discovered the source of all power.

22. All mistakes are but the mistakes of ignorance. Knowledge gaining and consequent power is what determines growth and evolution. The recognition and demonstration of knowledge is what constitutes power, and this power is spiritual power, and this spiritual power is the power which lies at the heart of all things; it is the soul of the universe.

23. This knowledge is the result of man's ability to think; thought is therefore the germ of man's conscious evolution. When man ceases to advance in his thoughts and ideals, his forces immediately begin to disintegrate and his countenance gradually registers these changing conditions.

24. Successful men make it their business to hold ideals of the conditions which they wish to realize. They constantly hold in mind the next step necessary to the ideal for which they are striving. Thoughts are the materials with which they build, and the imagination is their mental workshop. Mind is the ever- moving force with which they secure the persons and circumstances necessary to build their success structure, and imagination is the matrix in which all great things are fashioned.

25. If you have been faithful to your ideal, you will hear the call when circumstances are ready to materialize your plans and results will correspond in the exact ratio of your fidelity to your ideal. The ideal steadily held is what predetermines and attracts the necessary conditions for its fulfillment.

26. It is thus that you may weave a garment of spirit and power into the web of your entire existence; it is thus that you may lead a charmed life and be forever protected from all harm; it is thus that you may become a positive force whereby conditions of opulence and harmony may be attracted to you.

27. This is the leaven which is gradually permeating the general consciousness and is largely responsible for the conditions of unrest which are everywhere evident.

28. In the last Part, you created a mental image -- you brought it from the invisible into the visible. This week I want you to take an object and follow it back to its origination, see of what it really consists. If you do this you will develop imagination, insight, perception, and sagacity. These come not by the superficial observation of the multitude, but by a keen analytical observation which sees below the surface.

29. It is the few who know that the things which they see are only effects, and understand the causes by which these effects were brought into existence.

30. Take the same position as heretofore and visualize a Battleship. See the grim monster floating on the surface of the water; there appears to be no life anywhere about, all is silence. You know that by far the largest part of the vessel is under water, out of sight; you know that the ship is as large and as heavy as a twenty-story skyscraper; you know that there are hundreds of men ready to spring to their appointed task instantly; you know that every department is in charge of able, trained, skilled officials who have proven themselves competent to take charge of this marvelous piece of mechanism; you know that although it lies apparently oblivious to everything else, it has eyes which see everything for miles around, and nothing is permitted to escape its watchful vision; you know that while it appears quiet, submissive and innocent, it is prepared to hurl a steel projectile weighing thousands of pounds at an enemy many miles away; this and much more you can bring to mind with comparatively no effort whatever. But how did the battleship come to be where it is; how did it come into existence in the first place? All of this you want to know if you are a careful observer.

31. Follow the great steel plates through the foundries, see the thousands of men employed in their production. Go still further back, and see the ore as it comes from the mine, see it loaded on barges or cars, see it melted and properly treated; go back still further and see the architect and engineers who planned the vessel; let the thought carry you back still further in order to determine why they planned the vessel. You will see that you are now so far back that the vessel is something intangible, it no longer exists, it is now only a thought existing in the brain of the architect. But from where did the order come to plan the vessel? Probably from the Secretary of Defense, but probably this vessel was planned long before the war was thought of and that Congress had to pass a bill appropriating the money; possibly there was opposition, and speeches for or against the bill. Whom do these Congressmen represent? They represent you and me, so that our line of thought begins with the Battleship and ends with ourselves, and we find in the last analysis that our own thought is responsible for this and many other things of which we seldom think, and a little further reflection will develop the most important fact of all and that is, if someone had not discovered the law by which this tremendous mass of steel and iron could be made to float upon the water, instead of immediately going to the bottom, the battleship could not have come into existence at all.

32. This law is that, "the specific gravity of any substance is the weight of any volume of it, compared with an equal volume of water." The discovery of this law revolutionized every kind of ocean travel, commerce and warfare, and made the existence of the battleship, aircraft carriers, and cruise ships possible.

33. You will find exercises of this kind invaluable. When the thought has been trained to look below the surface everything takes on a different appearance: the insignificant becomes significant, the uninteresting interesting; the things which we supposed to be of no importance are seen to be the only really vital things in existence.

Look To This Day

For it is Life, the very Life of Life.

In Its brief course lie all the Verities and

Realities of your existence;

The Bliss of Growth;

The Glory of Action;

The Splendor of Beauty;

For Yesterday is but a Dream,

And tomorrow is only a Vision;

But Today well lived makes every

Yesterday a Dream of Happiness, and

Every Tomorrow a Vision of Hope.

Look well, therefore, to This Day!

- From the Sanskrit.

PART EIGHT Study Questions with Answers

71. What is the imagination? A form of constructive thought. The light by which we penetrate new worlds of thought and experience. The mighty instrument by which every inventor or discoverer opened the way from precedent to experience.

72. What is the result of imagination? The cultivation of the imagination leads to the development of the ideal out of which your future will emerge.

73. How may it be cultivated? By exercise; it must be supplied with nourishment or it cannot live.

74. How does imagination differ from daydreaming? Daydreaming is a form of mental dissipation, while imagination is a form of constructive thought which must precede every constructive action.

75. What are mistakes? The result of ignorance

76. What is knowledge? The result of man's ability to think.

77. What is the power with which successful men build? Mind is the very moving force with which they secure the persons and circumstances necessary to complete their plans.

78. What predetermines the result? The ideal held steadily in mind attracts the necessary conditions for its fulfillment.

79. What is the result of a keen analytical observation? The development of imagination, insight, perception and sagacity.

80. To what do these lead? Opulence and harmony.

INTRODUCTION - PART NINE

In this Part you may learn to fashion the tools by which you may build for yourself any condition you desire.

If you wish to change conditions you must change yourself. Your whims, your wishes, your fancies, your ambitions may be thwarted at every step, but your inmost thoughts will find expression just as certainly as the plant springs from the seed.

Suppose, then, we desire to change conditions, how are we to bring this about? The reply is simple: By the law of growth. Cause and effect are as absolute and undeviating in the hidden realm of thought as in the world of material things.

Hold in mind the condition desired; affirm it as an already existing fact. This indicates the value of a powerful affirmation. By constant repetition it becomes a part of ourselves. We are actually changing ourselves, are making ourselves what we want to be.

Character is not a thing of chance, but it is the result of continued effort. If you are timid, vacillating, self-conscious, or if you are over-anxious or harassed by thoughts of fear or impending danger, remember that is axiomatic that "two things cannot exist in the same place at the same time." Exactly the same thing is true in the mental and spiritual world, so that your remedy is plainly to substitute thoughts of courage, power, self-reliance and confidence for those of fear, lack and limitation.

The easiest and most natural way to do this is to select an affirmation which seems to fit your particular case. The positive thought will destroy the negative as certainly as light destroys darkness, and the results will be just as effectual.

Act is the blossom of thought, and conditions are the result of action, so that you constantly have in your possession the tools by which you will certainly and inevitably make or unmake yourself, and joy or suffering will be the reward.

PART NINE

1. There are only three things which can possibly be desired in the "world without" and each of them can be found in the "world within." The secret of finding them is simply to apply the proper "mechanism" of attachment to the omnipotent power to which each individual has access.

2. The three things which all mankind desires and which are necessary for his highest expression and complete development are Health, Wealth and Love. All will admit that Health is absolutely essential; no one can be happy if the physical body is in pain. All will not so readily admit that Wealth is necessary, but all must admit that a sufficient supply at least is necessary, and what would be considered sufficient for one, would be considered absolute and painful lack for another; and as Nature provides not only enough but abundantly, wastefully, lavishly, we realize that any lack or limitation is only the limitation which has been made by an artificial method of distribution.

3. All will probably admit that Love is the third, or maybe some will say the first essential necessary to the happiness of mankind; at any rate, those who possess all three, Health, Wealth, and Love, find nothing else which can be added to their cup of happiness.

4. We have found that the Universal substance is "All Health," "All Substance" and "All Love" and that the mechanism of attachment whereby we can consciously connect with this Infinite supply is in our method of thinking. To think correctly is therefore to enter into the "Secret Place of the Most High."

5. What shall we think? If we know this we shall have found the proper mechanism of attachment which will relate us to "Whatsoever things we desire." This mechanism may seem very simple when I give it to you, but read on. You will find that it is in reality the "Master-Key," the "Alladin's lamp," if you please; you will find that it is the foundation, the imperative condition, the absolute law of well-doing, which means well-being.

6. To think correctly, accurately, we must know the "Truth." The truth then is the underlying principle in every business or social relation. It is a condition precedent to every right action. To know the truth, to be sure, to be confident, affords a satisfaction beside which no other is at all comparable; it is the only solid ground in a world of doubt, conflict and danger.

7. To know the Truth is to be in harmony with the Infinite and Omnipotent power. To know the truth is, therefore, to connect yourself with a power which is irresistible and which will sweep away every kind of discord, inharmony, doubt or error of any kind, because the "Truth is mighty and will prevail."

8. The humblest intellect can readily foretell the result of any action when he knows that it is based on truth, but the mightiest intellect, the most profound and penetrating mind loses its way hopelessly and can form no conception of the results which may ensue when his hopes are based on a premise which he knows to be false.

9. Every action which is not in harmony with Truth, whether through ignorance or design, will result in discord and eventual loss in proportion to its extent and character.

10. How then are we to know the truth in order to attach this mechanism which will relate us to the Infinite?

11. We can make no mistake about this if we realize that truth is the vital principle of the Universal Mind and is Omnipresent. For instance, if you require health, a realization of the fact that the "I" in you is spiritual and that all spirit is one, that wherever a part is the whole must be, will bring about a condition of health, because every cell in the body must manifest the truth as you see it. If you see sickness, they will manifest sickness; if you see perfection they must manifest perfection. The affirmation, "I am whole, perfect, strong, powerful, loving, harmonious and happy", will bring about harmonious conditions. The reason for this is because the affirmation is in strict accordance with the Truth, and when truth appears every form of error or discord must necessarily disappear.

12. You have found that the "I" is spiritual. It must necessarily then always be no less than perfect. The affirmation "I am whole, perfect, strong, powerful, loving, harmonious and happy" is therefore an exact scientific statement.

13. Thought is a spiritual activity and spirit is creative, therefore the result of holding this thought in mind must necessarily bring about conditions in harmony with the thought.

14. If you require Wealth a realization of the fact that the "I" in you is one with the Universal mind which is all substance and is Omnipotent, will assist you in bringing into operation the law of attraction which will bring you into vibration with those forces which make for success and bring about conditions of power and affluence in direct proportion with the character and purpose of your affirmation.

15. Visualization is the mechanism of the attachment which you require. Visualization is a very different process from seeing. Seeing is physical, and is therefore related to the objective world, the "world without," but Visualization is a product of the imagination, and is therefore a product of the subjective mind, the "world within." It therefore possesses vitality; it will grow. The thing visualized will manifest itself in form. The mechanism is perfect. It was created by the Master Architect who "doeth all things well," but unfortunately sometimes the operator is inexperienced or inefficient, but practice and determination will overcome this defect.

16. If you require Love try to realize that the only way to get love is by giving it; that the more you give the more you will get, and the only way in which you can give it is to fill yourself with it, until you become a magnet. The method was explained in another lesson.

17. He who has learned to bring the greatest spiritual truths into touch with the so-called lesser things of life has discovered the secret of the solution of his problem. One is always quickened, made more thoughtful, by his nearness of approach to great ideas, great events, great natural objects, and great men. Lincoln is said to have begotten in all who came near him the feeling awakened when one approaches a mountain, and this sense asserts itself most keenly when one comes to realize that he has laid hold upon things that are eternal, the power of Truth.

18. It is sometimes an inspiration to hear from someone who has actually put these principles to the test, someone who has demonstrated them in their own life. A letter from Frederick Andrews offers the following insight:

19. I was about thirteen years old when Dr. T. W. Marsee, since passed over, said to my mother: "There is no possible chance, Mrs. Andrews. I lost my little boy the same way, after doing everything for him that it was possible to do. I have made a special study of these cases, and I know there is no possible chance for him to get well."

20. She turned to him and said: "Doctor, what would you do if he were your boy?" and he answered, "I would fight, fight, as long as there is a breath of life to fight for."

21. That was the beginning of a long drawn-out battle, with many ups and downs, the doctors all agreeing that there was no chance for a cure, though they encouraged and cheered us the best they could.

22. But at last the victory came, and I have grown from a little, crooked, twisted, cripple, going about on my hands and knees, to a strong, straight, well-formed man.

23. Now, I know you want the formula, and I will give it to you as briefly and quickly as I can.

24. I built up an affirmation for myself, taking the qualities I most needed and affirming for myself over and over again, "I am whole, perfect, strong, powerful, loving, harmonious and happy." I kept up this affirmation, always the same, never varying, till I could wake up in the night and find myself repeating, "I am whole, perfect, strong, powerful, loving, harmonious and happy." It was the last thing on my lips at night and the first thing in the morning.

25. Not only did I affirm it for myself, but for others that I knew needed it. I want to emphasize this point. Whatever you desire for yourself, affirm it for others, and it will help you both. We reap what we sow. If we send out thoughts of love and health, they return to us like bread cast upon the waters; but if we send out thoughts of fear, worry, jealousy, anger, hate, etc., we will reap the results in our own lives.

26. It used to be said that man is completely built over every seven years, but some scientists now declare that we build ourselves over entirely every eleven months; so we are really only eleven months old. If we build the defects back into our bodies year after year, we have no one to blame but ourselves.

27. Man is the sum total of his own thoughts, so the question is, how are we going to entertain only the good thoughts and reject the evil ones? At first we can't keep the evil thoughts from coming, but we can keep from entertaining them. The only way to do this is to forget them -- which means, get something for them. This is where the ready-made affirmation comes into play.

28. When a thought of anger, jealousy, fear or worry creeps in, just start your affirmation going. The way to fight darkness is with light -- the way to fight cold is with heat -- the way to overcome evils is with good. For myself, I never could find any help in denials. Affirm the good, and the bad will vanish. - Frederick Elias Andrews

29. If there is anything you require, it will be well for you to make use of this affirmation; it cannot be improved upon. Use it just as it is. Take it into the silence with you, until it sinks into your subconsciousness, so that you can use it anywhere: in your car, in the office, at home. This is the advantage of spiritual methods; they are always available. Spirit is omnipresent, every ready. All that is required is a proper recognition of its omnipotence, and a willingness or desire to become the recipient of its beneficent effects.

30. If our predominant mental attitude is one of power, courage, kindliness and sympathy, we shall find that our environment will reject conditions in correspondence with these thoughts; if it is weak, critical, envious and destructive, we shall find our environment reflecting conditions corresponding to these thoughts.

31. Thoughts are causes and conditions are effects. Herein is the explanation of the origin of both good and evil. Thought is creative and will automatically correlate with its object. This is a Cosmological law (a universal law), the law of Attraction, the law of Cause and Effect; the recognition and application of this law will determine both beginning and end; it is the law by which in all ages and in all times the people were led to believe in the power of prayer. "As thy faith is, so be it unto thee," is simply another, shorter and a better way of stating it.

32. This week visualize a plant. Take a flower, the one you most admire, bring it from the unseen into the seen, plant the tiny seed, water it, care for it, place it where it will get the direct rays of the morning sun, see the seed burst; it is now a living thing, something which is alive and beginning to search for the means of subsistence. See the roots penetrating the earth, watch them shoot out in all directions and remember that they are living cells dividing and subdividing, and that they will soon number millions, that each cell is intelligent, that it knows what is wants and knows how to get it. See the stem shoot forward and upward, watch it burst through the surface of the earth, see it divide and form branches, see how perfect and symmetrical each branch is formed, see the leaves begin to form, and then the tiny stems, each one holding aloft a bud, and as you watch you see the bud begin to unfold and your favorite flower comes to view. And now if you will concentrate intently you will become conscious of a fragrance; it is the fragrance of the flower as the breeze gently sways the beautiful creation which you have visualized.

33. When you are enabled to make your vision clear and complete you will be enabled to enter into the spirit of a thing. It will become very real to you. You will be learning to concentrate and the process is the same, whether you are concentrating on health, a favorite flower, an ideal, a complicated business proposition or any other problem of life.

34. Every success has been accomplished by persistent concentration upon the object in view.

PART NINE Study Questions with Answers

81. What is the imperative condition of all well-being? Well doing.

82. What is the condition precedent to every right action? Right thinking.

83. What is the underlying condition necessary in every business transaction or social relation? To know the Truth.

84. What is the result of a knowledge of the Truth? We can readily predict the result of any action that is based upon a true premise.

85. What is the result of any action based upon a false premise? We can form no conception of the results which may ensue.

86. How may we know the Truth? By a realization of the fact that Truth is the vital principle of the Universe and is therefore omnipresent.

87. What is the nature of Truth? It is spiritual.

88. What is the secret of the solution to every problem? To apply spiritual Truth.

89. What is the advantage of spiritual methods? They are always available.

90. What are the necessary requirements? A recognition of the omnipotence of spiritual power and a desire to become the recipient of its beneficent effects.

"Thought means life, since those who do not think do not live in any high or real sense. Thinking makes the man." - A. B. Alcott

INTRODUCTION - PART TEN

If you get a thorough understanding or the thought contained in Part Ten, you will have learned that nothing happens without a definite cause. You will be enabled to formulate your plans in accordance with exact knowledge. You will know how to control any situation by bringing adequate causes into play. When you win, as you will, you will know exactly why.

The ordinary man, who has no definite knowledge of cause and effect, is governed by his feelings or emotions. He thinks chiefly to justify his action. If he fails as a businessman, he says that luck is against him. If he dislikes music, he says that music is an expensive luxury. If he is a poor office man, he says that he could succeed better at some outdoor work. If he lacks friends, he says his individuality is too fine to be appreciated.

He never thinks his problem through to the end. In short, he does not know that every effect is the result of a certain definite cause, but he seeks to console himself with explanations and excuses. He thinks only in self-defense.

On the contrary, the man who understands that there is no effect without an adequate cause thinks impersonally. He gets down to bedrock facts regardless of consequences. He is free to follow the trail of truth wherever it may lead. He sees the issue clear to the end, and he meets the requirements fully and fairly, and the result is that the world gives him all that it has to give, in friendship, honor, love and approval.

PART TEN

1. Abundance is a natural law of the Universe. The evidence of this law is conclusive; we see it on every hand. Everywhere, Nature is lavish, wasteful, extravagant. Nowhere is economy observed in any created thing. Profusion is manifested in everything. The millions and millions of trees and flowers and plants and animals and the vast scheme of reproduction where the process of creating and recreating is forever going on, all indicates the lavishness with which Nature has made provision for man. That there is an abundance for everyone is evident, but that many fail to participate in this abundance is also evident. They have not yet come into a realization of the Universality of all substance, and that mind is the active principle whereby we are related to the things we desire.

2. All wealth is the offspring of power; possessions are of value only as they confer power. Events are significant only as they affect power; all things represent certain forms and degrees of power.

3. Knowledge of cause and effect as shown by the laws governing electricity, chemical affinity and gravitation, enables man to plan courageously and execute fearlessly. These laws are called Natural Laws, because they govern in the physical world, but all power is not physical power; there is also mental power, and there is moral and spiritual power.

4. Spiritual power is superior because it exists on a higher plane. It has enabled man to discover the law by which these wonderful forces of Nature could be harnessed and made to do the work of hundreds and thousands of men. It has enabled man to discover laws whereby time and space have been annihilated and the law of gravitation to be overcome. The operation of this law is dependent upon spiritual contact, as Henry Drummond well says:

5. "In the physical world as we know it, there exists the organic and the inorganic. The inorganic of the mineral world is absolutely cut off from the plant or animal world; the passage is hermetically sealed. These barriers have never yet been crossed. No change of substance, no modification of environment, no chemistry, no electricity, no form of energy, no evolution of any kind can ever endow a single atom of the mineral world with the attribute of Life."

6. "Only by the bending down into this dead world of some living form can those dead atoms be gifted with the properties of vitality; without this contact with life they remain fixed in the inorganic sphere forever. Huxley says that the doctrine of Biogenesis (or life only from life) is victorious all along the line, and Tyndall is compelled to say: 'I affirm that no shred of trustworthy evidence exists to prove that life in our day has ever appeared independent of antecedent life."

7. "Physical laws may explain the inorganic, Biology explains and accounts for the development of the organic, but of the point of contact Science is silent. A similar passage exists between the Natural world and the Spiritual world; this passage is

71

hermetically sealed on the natural side. The door is closed; no man can open it, no organic change, no mental energy, no moral effort, no progress of any kind can enable any human being to enter the spiritual world."

8. But as the plant reaches down into the mineral world and touches it with the mystery of Life, so the Universal Mind reaches down into the human mind and endows it with new, strange, wonderful and even marvelous qualities. All men or women who have ever accomplished anything in the world of industry, commerce or art have accomplished because of this process.

9. Thought is the connecting link between the Infinite and the finite, between the Universal and the individual. We have seen that there is an impassable barrier between the organic and the inorganic, and that the only way that matter can unfold is to be impregnated with life; as a seed reaches down into the mineral world and begins to unfold and reach out, the dead matter begins to live, a thousand invisible fingers begin to weave a suitable environment for the new arrival, and as the law of growth begins to take effect. We see the process continue until the Lily finally appears, and even "Solomon in all his glory was not arrayed like one of these".

10. Even so, a thought is dropped into the invisible substance of the Universal Mind, that substance from which all things are created, and as it takes root, the law of growth begins to take effect and we find that conditions and environment are but the objective form of our thought.

11. The law is that Thought is an active, vital form of dynamic energy which has the power to correlate with its object and bring it out of the invisible substance from which all things are created into the visible or objective world. This is the law by which, and through which all things come into manifestation; it is the Master Key by which you are admitted into the Secret Place of the Most High and are "given dominion over all things." With an understanding of this law you may "decree a thing and it shall be established unto thee."

12. It could not be otherwise. If the soul of the Universe as we know it is the Universal Spirit, then the Universe is simply the condition which the Universal Spirit has made for itself. We are simply individualized spirit and are creating the conditions for our growth in exactly the same way.

13. This creative power depends upon our recognition of the potential power of spirit or mind and must not be confused with Evolution. Creation is the calling into existence of that which does not exist in the objective world. Evolution is simply the unfolding of potentialities involved in things which already exist.

14. In taking advantage of the wonderful possibilities opened up to us through the operation of this law, we must remember that we ourselves contribute nothing to its efficacy as the Great Teacher said: "It is not I that doeth the works, but the Father that dwelleth in me, He doeth the work". We must take exactly the same position. We can do nothing to assist in the manifestation, we simply comply with the law, and the All-originating Mind will bring about the result.

15. The great error of the present day is the idea that Man has to originate the intelligence whereby the Infinite can proceed to bring about a specific purpose or result. Nothing of this kind is necessary; the Universal Mind can be depended upon to find the ways and means for bringing about any necessary manifestation. We must, however, create the ideal, and this ideal should be perfect.

16. We know that the laws governing Electricity have been formulated in such a way that this invisible power can be controlled and used for our benefit and comfort in thousands of ways. We know that messages are carried around the world, that ponderous machinery does its bidding, that it now illuminates practically the whole world, but we know too that if we consciously or ignorantly violate its law by touching a live wire when it is not properly insulated, the result will be unpleasant and possibly disastrous. A lack of understanding of the laws governing in the invisible world has the same result, and many are suffering the consequences all the time.

17. It has been explained that the law of causation depends upon polarity; a circuit must be formed. This circuit cannot be formed unless we operate in harmony with the law. How shall we operate in harmony with the law unless we know what the law is? How shall we know what the Law is? By study, by observation.

18. We see the law in operation everywhere. All nature testifies to the operation of the law by silently, constantly expressing itself in the law of growth. Where there is growth, there must be life; where there is life there must be harmony, so that everything that has life is constantly attracting to itself the conditions and the supply which are necessary for its most complete expression.

19. If your thought is in harmony with the creative Principle of Nature, it is in tune with the Infinite Mind, and it will form the circuit, it will not return to you void; but it is possible for you to think thoughts that are not in tune with the Infinite, and when there is no polarity, the circuit is not formed. What, then, is the result? What is the result when a dynamo is generating electricity, the circuit is cut off and there is no outlet? The dynamo stops.

20. It will be exactly the same with you, if you entertain thoughts which are not in accordance with the Infinite and cannot therefore be polarized; there is no circuit, you are isolated, the thoughts cling to you, harass you, worry you, and finally bring about disease and possibly death; the physician may not diagnose the case exactly in this way, he may give it some fancy name which has been manufactured for the various ills which are the result of wrong thinking, but the cause is the same nevertheless.

21. Constructive thought must necessarily be creative, but creative thought must be harmonious, and this eliminates all destructive or competitive thought. Wisdom, strength, courage and all harmonious conditions are the result of power and we have seen that all power is from within. Likewise, every lack, limitation or adverse circumstance is the result of weakness, and weakness is simply absence of power; it

73

comes from nowhere, it is nothing -- the remedy then is simply to develop power, and this is accomplished in exactly the same manner that all power is developed, by exercise.

22. This exercise consists in making an application of your knowledge. Knowledge will not apply itself. You must make the application. Abundance will not come to you out of the sky, neither will it drop into your lap, but a conscious realization of the law of attraction and the intention to bring it into operation for a certain, definite and specific purpose, and the will to carry out this purpose will bring about the materialization of your desire by a natural law of transference. If you are in business, it will increase and develop along regular channels, possibly new or unusual channels of distribution will be opened and when the law becomes fully operative, you will find that the things you seek are seeking you.

23. This week, select a blank space on the wall, or any other convenient spot, from where you usually sit. Mentally draw a black horizontal line about six inches long, try to see the line as plainly as though it were painted on the wall; now mentally draw two vertical lines connecting with this horizontal line at either end; now draw another horizontal line connecting with the two vertical lines; now you have a square. Try to see the square perfectly; when you can do so draw a circle within the square; now place a point in the center of the circle; now draw the point toward you about 10 inches; now you have a cone on a square base; you will remember that your work was all in black; change it to white, to red, to yellow.

24. If you can do this, you are making excellent progress and will soon be enabled to concentrate on any problem you may have in mind. When any object or purpose is clearly held in thought, its precipitation, in tangible and visible form, is merely a question of time.

"The vision always precedes and itself determines the realization." - Lillian Whiting

PART TEN Study Questions with Answers

91. What is Wealth? Wealth is the offspring of power.

92. Of what value are possessions? Possessions are of value only as they confer power.

93. Of what value is a knowledge of cause and effect? It enables men to plan courageously and execute fearlessly.

94. How does life originate in the inorganic world? Only by the introduction of some living form; there is no other way.

95. What is the connecting link between the finite and the Infinite? Thought is the connecting link.

96. Why is that so? Because the Universal can manifest only through the individual.

97. Upon what does causation depend? Upon polarity; a circuit must be formed; the Universal is the positive side of the battery of life, the individual is the negative, and thought forms the circuit.

98. Why do many fail to secure harmonious conditions? They do not understand the law; there is no polarity; they have not formed the circuit.

99. What is the remedy? A conscious recognition of the law of attraction with the intention of bring it into existence for a definite purpose.

100. What will be the result? Thought will correlate with its object and bring it into manifestation, because thought is a product of the spiritual man, and spirit is the creative Principle of the Universe.

"A vivid thought brings the power to paint it; and in proportion to the depth of its source is the force of its projection." - Emerson

INTRODUCTION - PART ELEVEN

Your life is governed by law - by actual, immutable principles that never vary. Law is in operation at all times, in all places. Fixed laws underlie all human actions. For this reason, men who control giant industries are enabled to determine with absolute precision just what percentage of every hundred thousand people will respond to any given set of conditions.

It is well, however, to remember that while every effect is the result of a cause, the effect in turn becomes a cause, which creates other effects, which in turn create still other causes; so that when you put the law of attraction into operation you must remember that you are starting a train of causation for good or otherwise which may have endless possibilities.

We frequently hear it said, "A very distressing situation came into my life, which could not have been the result of my thought, as I certainly never entertained any thought which could have such a result." We fail to remember that like attracts like in the mental world, and that the thought which we entertain brings to us certain friendships, companionships of a particular kind, and these in turn bring about conditions and environment, which in turn are responsible for the conditions of which we complain.

PART ELEVEN

1. Inductive reasoning is the process of the objective mind by which we compare a number of separate instances with one another until we see the common factor that gives rise to them all.

2. Induction proceeds by comparison of facts; it is this method of studying nature which has resulted in the discovery of a reign of law which has marked an epoch in human progress.

3. It is the dividing line between superstition and intelligence; it has eliminated the elements of uncertainty and caprice from men's lives and substituted law, reason, and certitude.

4. It is the "Watchman at the Gate" mentioned in a former lesson.

5. When, by virtue of this principle, the world to which the senses were accustomed had been revolutionized; when the sun had been arrested in his course, the apparently flat earth had been shaped into a ball and set whirling around him; when the inert matter had been resolved into active elements, and the universe presented itself wherever we directed the telescope and microscope, full of force, motion and life, we are constrained to ask by what possible means the delicate forms of organization in the midst of it are kept in order and repair.

6. Like poles and like forces repel themselves, or remain impenetrable to each other, and this cause seems in general sufficient to assign a proper place and distance to stars, men and forces. As men of different virtues enter into partnership, so do opposite poles attract each other. Elements that have no property in common, like acids and gases, cling to each other in preference and a general exchange is kept up between the surplus and the demand.

7. As the eye seeks and receives satisfaction from colors complementary to those which are given, so does need, want and desire, in the largest sense, induce, guide and determine action.

8. It is our privilege to become conscious of the principle and act in accordance with it. Cuvier sees a tooth belonging to an extinct race of animals. This tooth wants a body for the performance of its function, and it defines the peculiar body it stands in need of with such precision that Cuvier is able to reconstruct the frame of this animal.

9. Perturbations are observed in the motion of Uranus. Leverrier needs another star at a certain place to keep the solar system in order, and Neptune appears in the place and hour appointed.

10. The instinctive wants of the animal and the intellectual wants of Cuvier, the wants of nature and of the mind of Leverrier were alike, and thus the results: here the thoughts of an existence, there an existence. A well-defined, lawful want, therefore, furnishes the reason for the more complex operations of nature.

11. Having recorded correctly the answers furnished by nature and stretched our senses with the growing science over her surface; having joined hands with the levers that move the earth, we become conscious of such a close, varied and deep contact with the world without, that our wants and purposes become no less identified with the harmonious operations of this vast organization than the life, liberty, and happiness of the citizen is identified with the existence of his government.

12. As the interests of the individual are protected by the arms of the country, added to his own, and his needs may depend upon certain supply in the degree that they are felt more universally and steadily; in the same manner does conscious citizenship in the Republic of nature secure us from the annoyances of subordinate agents by alliance with superior powers, and by appeal to the fundamental laws of resistance or inducement offered to mechanical or chemical agents, distribute the labor to be performed between them and man to the best advantage of the inventor.

13. If Plato could have witnessed the pictures executed by the sun with the assistance of the photographer, or a hundred similar illustrations of what man does by induction, he would perhaps have been reminded of the intellectual midwifery of his master and, in his own mind might have arisen the vision of a land where all manual, mechanical labor and repetition is assigned to the power of nature, where our wants are satisfied by purely mental operations set in motion by the will, and where the supply is created by the demand.

14. However distant that land may appear, induction has taught men to make strides toward it and has surrounded him with benefits which are, at the same time, rewards for past fidelity and incentives for more assiduous devotion.

15. It is also an aid in concentrating and strengthening our faculties for the remaining part, giving unerring solution for individual as well as universal problems, by the mere operations of mind in the purest form.

16. Here we find a method, the spirit of which is to believe that what is sought has been

17. accomplished, in order to accomplish it; a method bequeathed upon us by the same Plato who, outside of this sphere, could never find how the ideas became realities.

18. This conception is also elaborated by Swedenborg in his doctrine of correspondences, and a still greater teacher has said, "What things so ever ye desire, when ye pray, believe that ye receive them, and ye shall have them." (Mark 11:24) The difference of the tenses in this passage is remarkable.

19. We are first to believe that our desire has already been fulfilled, its accomplishment will then follow. This is a concise direction for making use of the creative power of thought by impressing on the Universal subjective mind the particular thing which we desire as an already existing fact.

20. We are thus thinking on the plane of the absolute and eliminating all consideration of conditions or limitation and are planting a seed which, if left undisturbed, will finally germinate into external fruition.

21. To review: Inductive reasoning is the process of the objective mind, by which we compare a number of separate instances with one another until we see the common factor that gives rise to them all. We see people in every civilized country on the globe securing results by some process which they do not seem to understand themselves, and to which they usually attach more or less mystery. Our reason is given to us for the purpose of ascertaining the law by which these results are accomplished.

22. The operation of this thought process is seen in those fortunate natures that possess everything that others must acquire by toil, who never have a struggle with conscience because they always act correctly, and can never conduct themselves otherwise than with tact, learn everything easily, complete everything they begin with a happy knack, live in eternal harmony with themselves, without ever reflecting much what they do, or ever experiencing difficulty or toil.

23. The fruit of this thought is, as it were, a gift of the gods, but a gift which few as yet realize, appreciate, or understand. The recognition of the marvelous power which is possessed by the mind under proper conditions and the fact that this power can be utilized, directed, and made available for the solution of every human problem is of transcendental importance.

24. All truth is the same, whether stated in modern scientific terms or in the language of apostolic times. There are timid souls who fail to realize that the very completeness of truth requires various statements -- that no one human formula will show every side of it.

25. Changing, emphasis, new language, novel interpretations, unfamiliar perspectives, are not, as some suppose, signs of departure from truth but on the contrary, they are evidence that the truth is being apprehended in new relations to human needs, and is becoming more generally understood.

26. The truth must be told to each generation and to every people in new and different terms, so that when the Great Teacher said -- "Believe that ye receive and ye shall receive" or, when Paul said -- "Faith is the substance of things hoped for, the evidence of things not seen" or, when modern science says -- "The law of attraction is the law by which thought correlates with its object", each statement when subjected to analysis is found to contain exactly the same truth, the only difference being in the form of presentation.

27. We are standing on the threshold of a new era. The time has arrived when man has learned the secrets of mastery and the way is being prepared for a new social order, more wonderful than anything ever heretofore dreamed of. The conflict of modern science with theology, the study of comparative religions, the tremendous power of new social movements, all of these are but clearing the way for the new order. They may have destroyed traditional forms which have become antiquated and impotent, but nothing of value has been lost.

28. A new faith has been born, a faith which demands a new form of expression, and this faith is taking form in a deep consciousness of power which is being manifested, in the present spiritual activity found on every hand.

29. The spirit which sleeps in the mineral, breathes in the vegetable, moves in the animal and reaches its highest development in man is the Universal Mind, and it behooves us to span the gulf between being and doing, theory and practice, by demonstrating our understanding of the dominion which we have been given.

30. By far the greatest discovery of all the centuries is the power of thought. The importance of this discovery has been a little slow in reaching the general consciousness, but it has arrived, and already in every field of research the importance of this greatest of all great discoveries is being demonstrated.

31. You ask in what does the creative power of thought consist? It consists in creating ideas, and these in turn objectify themselves by appropriating, inventing, observing, discerning, discovering, analyzing, ruling, governing, combining, and applying matter and force. It can do this because it is an intelligent creative power.

32. Thought reaches its loftiest activity when plunged into its own mysterious depth; when it breaks through the narrow compass of self and passes from truth to truth to the region of eternal light, where all which is, was or ever will be melt into one grand harmony.

33. From this process of self-contemplation comes inspiration which is creative intelligence, and which is undeniably superior to every element, force or law of nature, because it can understand, modify, govern and apply them to its own ends and purposes and therefore possess them.

34. Wisdom begins with the dawn of reason, and reason is but an understanding of the knowledge and principles whereby we may know the true meaning of things. Wisdom, then, is illuminated reason, and this wisdom leads to humility, for humility is a large part of Wisdom.

35. We all know many who have achieved the seemingly impossible, who have realized life-long dreams, who have changed everything including themselves. We have sometimes marveled at the demonstration of an apparently irresistible power, which seemed to be ever available just when it was most needed, but it is all clear now. All that is required is an understanding of certain definite fundamental principles and their proper application.

36. For your exercise this week, concentrate on the quotation taken from the Bible, "Whatsoever things ye desire, when ye pray, believe that ye receive them and ye shall have them". Notice that there is no limitation, "Whatsoever things" is very definite and implies that the only limitation which is placed upon us in our ability to think, to be equal to the occasion, to rise to the emergency, to remember that Faith is not a shadow, but a substance, "the substance of things hoped for, the evidence of things not seen."

"Death is but the natural process whereby all material forms are thrown into the crucible for reproduction in fresh diversity."

PART ELEVEN Study Questions with Answers

101. What is inductive reasoning? The process of the objective mind by which we compare a number of separate instances with each other until we see the common factor which gives rise to them all.

102. What has this method of studying accomplished? It has resulted in the discovery of a reign of law which has marked an epoch in human progress.

103. What is it that guides and determines action? It is need, want and desire which in the largest sense induce, guide and determine action.

104. What is the formula for the unerring solution of every individual problem? We are to believe that our desire has already been fulfilled; its accomplishment will then follow.

105. What great Teachers advocated it? Jesus, Plato, Swedenborg.

106. What is the result of this thought process? We are thinking on the plane of the absolute and planting a seed, which if left undisturbed will germinate into fruition.

107. Why is it scientifically exact? Because it is Natural Law.

108. What is Faith? "Faith is the substance of things hoped for, the evidence of things unseen."

109. What is the Law of Attraction? The Law by which Faith is brought into manifestation.

110. What importance do you attach to an understanding of this law? It has eliminated the elements of uncertainty and caprice from men's lives and substituted law, reason, and certitude.

INTRODUCTION - PART TWELVE

Part Twelve is enclosed herewith. In the fourth paragraph you will find the following statement: "You must first have the knowledge of your power; second, the courage to dare; third, the faith to do."

If you concentrate upon the thoughts given, if you give them your entire attention, you will find a world of meaning in each sentence, and will attract to yourself other thoughts in harmony with them, and you will soon grasp the full significance of the vital knowledge upon which you are concentrating.

Knowledge does not apply itself; we as individuals must make the application, and the application consists in fertilizing the thought with a living purpose.

The time and thought which most persons waste in aimless effort would accomplish wonders if properly directed with some special object in view. In order to do this, it is necessary to center your mental force upon a specific thought and hold it there, to the exclusion of all other thoughts. If you have ever looked through the viewfinder on a videocamera, you found that when the object was not in focus, the impression was indistinct and possibly blurred, but when the proper focus was obtained the picture was clear and distinct. This illustrates the power of concentration. Unless you can concentrate upon the object which you have in view, you will have but a hazy, indifferent, vague, indistinct and blurred outline of your ideal and the results will be in accordance with your mental picture.

PART TWELVE

1. There is no purpose in life that cannot be best accomplished through a scientific understanding of the creative power of thought.

2. This power to think is common to all. Man is, because he thinks. Man's power to think is infinite; consequently his creative power is unlimited.

3. We know that thought is building for us the thing we think of and actually bringing it nearer, yet we find it difficult to banish fear, anxiety or discouragement, all of which are powerful thought forces, and which continually send the things we desire further away, so that it is often one step forward and two steps backward.

4. The only way to keep from going backward is to keep going forward. Eternal vigilance is the price of success. There are three steps, and each one is absolutely essential. You must first have the knowledge of your power; second, the courage to dare; third, the faith to do.

5. With this as a basis you can construct an ideal business, an ideal home, ideal friends, and an ideal environment. You are not restricted as to material or cost. Thought is omnipotent and has the power to draw on the Infinite bank of primary substance for all that it requires. Infinite resources are therefore at your command.

6. But your ideal must be sharp, clear-cut, definite. To have one ideal today, another tomorrow, and a third next week, means to scatter your forces and accomplish nothing; your result will be a meaningless and chaotic combination of wasted material.

7. Unfortunately this is the result which many are securing, and the cause is self evident. If a sculptor started out with a piece of marble and a chisel and changed his ideal every fifteen minutes, what result could he expect? And why should you expect any different result in molding the greatest and most plastic of all substances, the only real substance?

8. The result of this indecision and negative thought is often found in the loss of material wealth. Supposed independence which required many years of toil and effort suddenly disappears. It is often found then that money and property are not independence at all. On the contrary, the only independence is found to be a practical working knowledge of the creative power of thought.

9. This practical working method cannot come to you until you learn that the only real power which you can have is the power to adjust yourself to Divine and unchangeable principles. You cannot change the Infinite, but you can come into an understanding of Natural laws. The reward of this understanding is a conscious realization of your ability to adjust your thought faculties with the Universal Thought which is Omnipresent. Your ability to cooperate with this Omnipotence will indicate the degree of success with which you meet.

10. The power of thought has many counterfeits which are more or less fascinating, but the results are harmful instead of helpful.

11. Of course, worry, fear, and all negative thoughts produce a crop after their kind; those who harbor thoughts of this kind must inevitably reap what they have sown.

12. Again, there are the Phenomena seekers who gormandize on the so-called proofs and demonstration obtained at materializing seances. They throw open their mental doors and soak themselves in the most poisonous currents which can be found in the psychic world. They do not seem to understand that it is the ability to become negative, receptive and passive, and thus drain themselves of all their vital force, which enables them to bring about these vibratory thought forms.

13. There are also the Hindu worshippers, who see in the materializing phenomena which are performed by the so-called adepts, a source of power, forgetting, or never seeming to realize that as soon as the will is withdrawn the forms wither, and the vibratory forces of which they are composed vanish.

14. Telepathy, or thought transference, has received considerable attention, but as it requires a negative mental state on the part of the receiver, the practice is harmful. A thought may be sent with the intention of hearing or seeing, but it will bring the penalty attached to the inversion of the principle involved.

15. In many instances, hypnotism is positively dangerous to the subject as well as the operator. No one familiar with the laws governing in the mental world would think of attempting to dominate the will of another, for by so doing, he will gradually (but surely) divest himself of his own power.

16. All of these perversions have their temporary satisfaction and for some, a keen fascination, but there is an infinitely greater fascination in a true understanding of the world of power within, a power which increases with use, is permanent instead of fleeing, which not only is potent as a remedial agency to bring about the remedy for past error or results of wrong thinking, but is a prophylactic agency protecting us from all manner and form of danger, and finally is an actual creative force with which we can build new conditions and new environment.

17. The law is that thought will correlate with its object and bring forth in the material world the correspondence of the thing thought or produced in the mental world. We then discern the absolute necessity of seeing that every thought has the inherent germ of truth in order that the law of growth will bring into manifestation good, for good alone can confer any permanent power.

18. The principle which gives the thought the dynamic power to correlate with its object, and therefore to master every adverse human experience, is the law of attraction, which is another name for love. This is an eternal and fundamental principle, inherent in all things, in every system of Philosophy, in every Religion, and in every Science. There is no getting away from the law of love. It is feeling that imparts vitality to thought. Feeling is desire, and desire is love. Thought impregnated with love becomes invincible.

19. We find this truth emphasized wherever the power of thought is understood. The Universal Mind is not only Intelligence, but it is substance, and this substance is the

attractive force which brings electrons together by the law of attraction so that they form atoms. The atoms in turn are brought together by the same law and form molecules; molecules take objective forms. And so we find that the law of love is the creative force behind every manifestation, not only of atoms, but of worlds, of the Universe, of everything of which the imagination can form any conception.

20. It is the operation of this marvelous law of attraction which has caused men in all ages and all times to believe that there must be some personal being who responded to their petitions and desires, and manipulated events in order to comply with their requirements.

21. It is the combination of Thought and Love which forms the irresistible force, called the law of attraction. All natural laws are irresistible. The law of Gravitation, or Electricity, or any other law operates with mathematical exactitude. There is no variation; it is only the channel of distribution which may be imperfect. If a bridge falls, we do not attribute the collapse to any variation of the law of gravitation. If a light fails us, we do not conclude that the laws governing electricity cannot be depended upon, and if the law of attraction seems to be imperfectly demonstrated by an inexperienced or uninformed person, we are not to conclude that the greatest and most infallible law upon which the entire system of creation depends has been suspended. We should rather conclude that a little more understanding of the law is required, for the same reason that a correct solution of a difficult problem in Mathematics is not always readily and easily obtained.

22. Things are created in the mental or spiritual world before they appear in the outward act or event. By the simple process of governing our thought forces today, we help create the events which will come into our lives in the future, perhaps even tomorrow. Educated desire is the most potent means of bringing into action the law of attraction.

23. Man is so constituted that he must first create the tools, or implements by which he gains the power to think. The mind cannot comprehend an entirely new idea until a corresponding vibratory brain cell has been prepared to receive it. This explains why it is so difficult for us to receive or appreciate an entirely new idea; we have no brain cell capable of receiving it. We are therefore incredulous; we do not believe it.

24. If, therefore, you have not been familiar with the Omnipotence of the law of attraction, and the scientific method by which it can be put into operation, or if you have not been familiar with the unlimited possibilities which it opens to those who are enabled to take advantage of the resources it offers, begin now and create the necessary brain cells which will enable you to comprehend the unlimited powers which may be yours by cooperating with Natural Law. This is done by concentration or attention.

25. The intention governs the attention. Power comes through repose. It is by concentration that deep thoughts, wise speech, and all forces of high potentiality are accomplished.

26. It is in the Silence that you get into touch with the Omnipotent power of the subconscious mind from which all power is evolved.

27. He who desires wisdom, power, or permanent success of any kind will find it only within; it is an unfoldment. The unthinking may conclude that the silence is very simple and easily attained, but it should be remembered that only in absolute silence may one come into contact with Divinity itself, may learn of the unchangeable law and open for himself the channels by which persistent practice and concentration lead to perfection.

28. This week go to the same room, take the same chair, the same position as previously. Be sure to relax, let go, both mentally and physically. Always do this; never try to do any mental work under pressure. See that there are no tense muscles or nerves, that you are entirely comfortable. Now realize your unity with omnipotence; get into touch with this power, come into a deep and vital understanding, appreciation, and realization of the fact that your ability to think is your ability to act upon the Universal Mind and bring it into manifestation. Realize that it will meet any and every requirement, that you have exactly the same potential ability which any individual ever did have or ever will have, because each is but an expression or manifestation of the One. All are parts of the whole; there is no difference in kind or quality, the only difference being one of degree.

"Thought cannot conceive of anything that may not be brought to expression. He who first uttered it may be only the suggester, but the doer will appear." - Wilson.

PART TWELVE Study Questions with Answers

111. How may any purpose in life be best accomplished? Through a scientific understanding of the spiritual nature of thought.

112. What three steps are absolutely essential? The knowledge of our power, the courage to dare, the faith to do.

113. How is the practical working knowledge secured? By an understanding of Natural laws.

114. What is the reward of an understanding of these laws? A conscious realization of our ability to adjust ourselves to Divine and unchanging principles.

115. What will indicate the degree of success with which we meet? The degree in which we realize that we cannot change the Infinite but must cooperate with it.

116. What is the principle which gives thought its dynamic power? The Law of Attraction which rests on vibration, which in turn rests upon the law of love. Thought impregnated with love becomes invincible.

117. Why is this law irresistible? Because it is a Natural law. All Natural laws are irresistible and unchangeable and act with mathematical exactitude. There is no deviation or variation.

118. Why then does it sometimes seem to be difficult to find the solution to our problems in life? For the same reason that it is sometimes difficult to find the correct solution to a difficult mathematical problem. The operator is uninformed or inexperienced.

119. Why is it impossible for the mind to grasp an entirely new idea? We have no corresponding vibratory brain cell capable of receiving the idea.

120. How is wisdom secured? By concentration; it is an unfoldment; it comes from within.

INTRODUCTION - PART THIRTEEN

Physical science is responsible for the marvelous age of invention in which we are now living, but spiritual science is now setting out on a career whose possibilities no one can foretell.

Spiritual science has previously been the football of the uneducated, the superstitious, the mystical, but men are now interested in definite methods and demonstrated facts only.

We have come to know that thinking is a spiritual process, that vision and imagination preceded action and event, that the day of the dreamer has come. The following lines by Mr. Herbert Kaufman are interesting in this connection.

"They are the architects of greatness, their vision lies within their souls, they peer beyond the veils and mists of doubt and pierce the walls of unborn Time. The belted wheel, the trail of steel, the churning screw, are shuttles in the loom on which they weave their magic tapestries. Makers of Empire, they have fought for bigger things than crowns and higher seats than thrones. Your homes are set upon the land a dreamer found. The pictures on its walls are visions from a dreamer's soul.

They are the chose few -- the blazers of the way. Walls crumble and Empires fall, the tidal wave sweeps from the sea and tears a fortress from its rocks. The rotting nations drop off from Time's bough, and only things the dreamers make live on."

Part Thirteen which follows tells why the dreams of the dreamer come true. It explains the law of causation by which dreamers, inventors, authors, financiers, bring about the realization of their desires. It explains the law by which the thing pictured upon our mind eventually becomes our own.

PART THIRTEEN

1. It has been the tendency, and, as might be proved, a necessity for science to seek the explanation of everyday facts by a generalization of those others which are less frequent and form the exception. Thus does the eruption of the volcano manifest the heat which is continually at work in the interior of the earth and to which the latter owes much of her configuration.

2. Thus does the lightning reveal a subtle power constantly busy to produce changes in the inorganic world, and, as dead languages now seldom heard were once ruling among the nations, so does a giant tooth in Siberia, or a fossil in the depth of the earth, not only bear record of the evolution of past ages, but thereby explains to us the origin of the hills and valleys which we inhabit today.

3. In this way a generalization of facts which are rare, strange, or form the exception, has been the magnetic needle guiding to all the discoveries of inductive science.

4. This method is founded upon reason and experience and thereby destroyed superstition, precedent and conventionality.

5. It is almost three-hundred years since Lord Bacon recommended this method of study, to which the civilized nations owe the greater part of their prosperity and the more valuable part of their knowledge; purging the mind from narrow prejudices, denominated theories, more effectually than by the keenest irony; calling the attention of men from heaven to earth more successfully by surprising experiments than by the most forcible demonstration of their ignorance; educating the inventive faculties more powerfully by the near prospect of useful discoveries thrown open to all, than by talk of bringing to light the innate laws of our mind.

6. The method of Bacon has seized the spirit and aim of the great philosophers of Greece and carried them into effect by the new means of observation which another age offered; thus gradually revealing a wondrous field of knowledge in the infinite space of astronomy, in the microscopic egg of embryology, and the dim age of geology; disclosing an order of the pulse which the logic of Aristotle could never have unveiled, and analyzing into formerly unknown elements the material combinations which no dialectic of the scholastics could force apart.

7. It has lengthened life; it has mitigated pain; it has extinguished diseases; it has increased the fertility of the soil; it has given new securities to the mariner; it has spanned great rivers with bridges of form unknown to our fathers; it has guided the thunderbolt from heaven to earth; it has lighted up night with the splendor of day; it has extended the range of human vision; it has multiplied the power of the human muscles; it has accelerated motion; it has annihilated distance; it has facilitated intercourse, correspondence, all friendly offices, all dispatch of business; it has enabled men to descend into the depths of the sea, to soar into the air, to penetrate securely into the noxious recesses of the earth.

8. This then is the true nature and scope of induction. But the greater the success which men have achieved in the inductive science, the more does the whole tenor of their teachings and example impress us with the necessity of observing carefully, patiently, accurately, with all the instruments and resources at our command the individual facts before venturing upon a statement of general laws.

9. To ascertain the bearing of the spark drawn from the electric machine under every variety of circumstances, that we thus may be emboldened with Franklin to address, in the form of a kite, the question to the cloud about the nature of the lightning. To assure ourselves of the manner in which bodies fall with the exactness of a Galileo, that with Newton we may dare to ask the moon about the force that fastens it to the earth.

10. In short, by the value we set upon truth, by our hope in a steady and universal progress, not to permit a tyrannical prejudice to neglect or mutilate unwelcome facts, but to rear the superstructure of science upon the broad and unchangeable basis of full attention paid to the most isolated as well as the most frequent phenomena.

11. An ever-increasing material may be collected by observation, but the accumulated facts are of very different value for the explanation of nature, and as we esteem most highly those useful qualities of men which are of the rarest occurrence, so does natural philosophy sift the facts and attach a pre-eminent importance to that striking class which cannot be accounted for by the usual and daily observation of life.

12. If then, we find that certain persons seem to possess unusual power, what are we to conclude? First, we may say, it is not so, which is simply an acknowledgment of our lack of information because every honest investigator admits that there are many strange and previously unaccountable phenomena constantly taking place. Those, however, who become acquainted with the creative power of thought, will no longer consider them unaccountable.

13. Second, we may say that they are the result of supernatural interference, but a scientific understanding of Natural Laws will convince us that there is nothing supernatural. Every phenomenon is the result of an accurate definite cause, and the cause is an immutable law or principle which operates with invariable precision, whether the law is put into operation consciously or unconsciously.

14. Third, we may say that we are on "forbidden ground," that there are some things which we should not know. This objection was used against every advance in human knowledge. Every individual who ever advanced a new idea, whether a Columbus, a Darwin, a Galileo, a Fulton or an Emerson, was subjected to ridicule or persecution; so that this objection should receive no serious consideration, but on the contrary, we should carefully consider every fact which is brought to our attention. By doing this we will more readily ascertain the law upon which it is based.

15. It will be found that the creative power of thought will explain every possible condition or experience, whether physical, mental or spiritual.

16. Thought will bring about conditions in correspondence with the predominant mental attitude. Therefore, if we fear disaster, as fear is a powerful form of thought, disaster will be the certain result of our thinking. It is this form of thought which frequently sweeps away the result of many years of toil and effort.

17. If we think of some form of material wealth we may secure it. By concentrated thought the required conditions will be brought about, and the proper effort put forth, which will result in bringing about the circumstances necessary to realize our desires; but we often find that when we secure the things we thought we wanted, they do not have the effect we expected. That is, the satisfaction is only temporary, or possibly is the reverse of what we expected.

18. What, then, is the proper method of procedure? What are we to think in order to secure what we really desire? What you and I desire, what we all desire, what every one is seeking, is Happiness and Harmony. If we can be truly happy we shall have everything the world can give. If we are happy ourselves, we can make others happy.

19. But we cannot be happy unless we have, health, strength, congenial friends, pleasant environment, sufficient supply, not only to take care of our necessities but to provide for those comforts and luxuries to which we are entitled.

20. The old orthodox way of thinking was to be "a worm," to be satisfied with our portion whatever it is; but the modern idea is to know that we are entitled to the best of everything, that the "Father and I are one" and that the "Father" is the Universal Mind, the Creator, the Original Substance from which all things proceed.

21. Now admitting that this is all true in theory, and it has been taught for two thousand years, and is the essence of every system of Philosophy or Religion, how are we to make it practical in our lives? How are we to get the actual, tangible results here and now?

22. In the first place, we must put our knowledge into practice. Nothing can be accomplished in any other way. The athlete may read books and lessons on physical training all his life, but unless he begins to give out strength by actual work he will never receive any strength; he will eventually get exactly what he gives, but he will have to give it first. It is exactly the same with us. We will get exactly what we give, but we shall have to give it first. It will then return to us many fold, and the giving is simply a mental process, because thoughts are causes and conditions are effects; therefore in giving thoughts of courage, inspiration, health or help of any kind we are setting causes in motion which will bring about their effect.

23. Thought is a spiritual activity and is therefore creative, but make no mistake: thought will create nothing unless it is consciously, systematically, and constructively directed; and herein is the difference between idle thinking, which is simply a dissipation of effort, and constructive thinking, which means practically unlimited achievement.

24. We have found that everything we get comes to us by the Law of Attraction. A happy thought cannot exist in an unhappy consciousness, therefore the consciousness must change, and, as the consciousness changes, all conditions necessary to meet the changed consciousness must gradually change, in order to meet the requirements of the

new situation.

25. In creating a Mental Image or an Ideal, we are projecting a thought into the Universal Substance from which all things are created. This Universal Substance is Omnipresent, Omnipotent and Omniscient. Are we to inform the Omniscient as to the proper channel to be used to materialize our demand? Can the finite advise the Infinite? This is the cause of failure, of every failure. We recognize the Omnipresence of the Universal Substance, but we fail to appreciate the fact that this substance is not only Omnipresent, but is Omnipotent and Omniscient, and consequently will set causes in motion concerning which we may be entirely ignorant.

26. We can best conserve our interests by recognizing the Infinite Power and Infinite Wisdom of the Universal Mind, and in this way become a channel whereby the Infinite can bring about the realization of our desire. This means that recognition brings about realization. Therefore, for your exercise this week, make use of the principle, recognize the fact that you are a part of the whole, and that a part must be the same in kind and quality as the whole; the only difference there can possibly be is in degree.

27. When this tremendous fact begins to permeate your consciousness, when you really come into a realization of the fact that you (not your body, but the Ego), the "I," the spirit which thinks is an integral part of the great whole, that it is the same in substance, in quality, in kind, that the Creator could create nothing different from Himself, you will also be able to say, "The Father and I are one" and you will come into an understanding of the beauty, the grandeur, the transcendental opportunities which have been placed at your disposal.

"Increase in me that wisdom

Which discovers my truest interest,

Strengthen my resolution

To perform that which wisdom dictates." - Franklin

PART THIRTEEN Study Questions with Answers

121. What is the method by which natural philosophers obtain and apply their knowledge? To observe individual facts carefully, patiently, accurately, with all the instruments and resources at their command, before venturing upon a statement of general laws.

122. How may we be certain that this method is correct? By not permitting a tyrannical prejudice to neglect or mutilate unwelcome facts.

123. What class of facts are esteemed most highly? Those which cannot be accounted for by the usual daily observation of life.

124. Upon what is this principle founded? Upon reason and experience.

125. What does it destroy? Superstition, precedent and conventionality.

126. How have these laws been discovered? By a generalization of facts which are uncommon, rare, strange and form the exception.

127. How may we account for much of the strange and heretofore unexplainable phenomena which is constantly taking place? By the creative power of thought.

128. Why is this so? Because when we learn of a fact, we can be sure that it is the result of a certain definite cause and that this cause will operate with invariable precision.

129. What is the result of this knowledge? It will explain the cause of every possible condition, whether physical, mental or spiritual.

130. How will our best interest be conserved? By a recognition of the fact that a knowledge of the creative nature of thought puts us in touch with Infinite power.

INTRODUCTION - PART FOURTEEN

You have found from your study thus far that thought is a spiritual activity and is therefore endowed with creative power. This does not mean that some thought is creative, but that all thought is creative. This same principle can be brought into operation in a negative way, through the process of denial.

The conscious and subconscious are but two phases of action in connection with one mind. The relation of the subconscious to the conscious is quite analogous to that existing between a weather vane and the atmosphere. Just as the least pressure of the atmosphere causes an action on the part of the weather vane, so does the least thought entertained by the conscious mind produce within your subconscious mind action in exact proportion to the depth of feeling characterizing the thought and the intensity with which the thought is indulged.

It follows that if you deny unsatisfactory conditions, you are withdrawing the creative power of your thought from these conditions. You are cutting them away at the root. You are sapping their vitality.

Remember that the law of growth necessarily governs every manifestation in the objective, so that a denial of unsatisfactory conditions will not bring about instant change. A plant will remain visible for some time after its roots have been cut, but it will gradually fade away and eventually disappear; so the withdrawal of your thought from the contemplation of unsatisfactory conditions will gradually, but surely, terminate these conditions.

You will see that this is an exactly opposite course from the one which we would naturally be inclined to adopt. It will therefore have an exactly opposite effect to the one usually secured. Most persons concentrate intently upon unsatisfactory conditions, thereby giving the condition that measure of energy and vitality which is necessary in order to supply a vigorous growth.

PART FOURTEEN

1. The Universal Energy in which all motion, light, heat, and color have their origin, does not partake of the limitation of the many effects of which it is the cause, but it is supreme over them all. This Universal Substance is the source of all Power, Wisdom and Intelligence.

2. To recognize this Intelligence is to acquaint yourself with the knowing quality of Mind and through it to move upon the Universal Substance, and bring it into harmonious relations in your affairs.

3. This is something that the most learned physical science teacher has not attempted -- a field of discovery upon which he has not yet launched; in fact, but few of the materialistic schools have ever caught the first ray of this light. It does not seem to have dawned upon them that wisdom is just as much present everywhere as are force and substance.

4. Some will say: if these principles are true, why are we not demonstrating them? As the fundamental principle is obviously correct, why do we not get proper results? We do. We get results in exact accordance with our understanding of the law and our ability to make the proper application. We secured no results from the laws governing electricity until someone formulated the law and showed us how to apply it.

5. This puts us in an entirely new relation to our environment, opening up possibilities previously undreamed of, and this by an orderly sequence of law which is naturally involved in our new mental attitude.

6. Mind is creative and the principle upon which this law is based is sound and legitimate

7. and is inherent in the nature of things; but this creative power does not originate in the individual, but in the Universal, which is the source and fountain of all energy and substance, the individual is simply the channel for the distribution of this energy. The individual is the means by which the Universal produces the various combinations which result in the formation of phenomena.

8. We know that scientists have resolved matter into an immense number of molecules. These molecules have been resolved into atoms, and the atoms into electrons. The discovery of electrons in high vacuum glass tubes containing fused terminals of hard metal, indicates conclusively that these electrons fill all space; that they exist everywhere, that they are omnipresent. They fill all material bodies and occupy the whole of what we call empty space. This, then, is the Universal Substance from which all things proceed.

9. Electrons would forever remain electrons unless directed where to go to be assembled into atoms and molecules, and this director is Mind. A number of electrons revolving around a center of force constitute an atom. Atoms unite in absolutely regular mathematical ratios and form molecules, and these unite with each other to form a multitude of compounds which unite to build the Universe.

10. The lightest known atom is hydrogen and this is 1,700 times heavier than an electron. An atom of mercury is 300,000 times heavier than an electron. Electrons are pure negative electricity, and as they have the same potential velocity as all other cosmic energy, such as heat, light, electricity and thought (189,380 miles per second), neither time nor space require consideration. The manner in which the velocity of light was ascertained is interesting.

11. The velocity of light was obtained by the Danish astronomer Roemer in 1676, by observing the eclipses of Jupiter's moons. When the earth was nearest to Jupiter, the eclipse appeared about eight and one-half minutes too soon for the calculations, and when the earth was most remote from Jupiter, they were about eight and one-half minutes too late. Roemer concluded the reason to be that it required 17 minutes for light from the planet to traverse the diameter of the earth's orbit, which measured the difference of the distances of the earth from Jupiter. This calculation has since been verified, and proves that light travels about 186,000 miles a second.

12. Electrons manifest in the body as cells, and possess mind and intelligence sufficient for them to perform their functions in the human physical anatomy. Every part of the body is composed of cells, some of which operate independently, others in communities. Some are busy building tissue, while others are engaged in forming the various secretions necessary for the body. Some act as carriers of material; others are the surgeons whose work it is to repair damage; others are scavengers, carrying off waste; others are constantly ready to repel invaders or other undesirable intruders of the germ family.

13. All these cells are moving for a common purpose and each one is not only a living organism, but has sufficient intelligence to enable it to perform its necessary duties. It is also endowed with sufficient intelligence to conserve the energies and perpetuate its own life. It must, therefore, secure sufficient nourishment and it has been found that it exercises choice in the selection of such nourishment.

14. Each cell is born, reproduces itself, dies and is absorbed. The maintenance of health and life itself depends upon the constant regeneration of these cells.

15. It is therefore apparent that there is mind in every atom of the body. This mind is negative mind, and the power of the individual to think makes him positive, so that he can control this negative mind. This is the scientific explanation for metaphysical healing, and will enable anyone to understand the principle upon which this remarkable phenomenon rests.

16. This negative mind, which is contained in every cell of the body, has been called the subconscious mind because it acts without our conscious knowledge. We have found that this subconscious mind is responsive to the will of the conscious mind.

17. All things have their origin in mind, and appearances are the result of thought. So that we see that things in themselves have no origin, permanency, or reality. Since they are produced by thought, they can be erased by thought.

18. In mental as in natural science, experiments are being made and each discovery lifts man one step higher toward his possible goal. We find that every man is the reflection of the thought he has entertained during his lifetime. This is stamped on his face, his form, his character, his environment.

19. Back of every effect there is a cause, and if we follow the trail to its starting point, we shall find the creative principle out of which it grew. Proofs of this are now so complete that this truth is generally accepted.

20. The objective world is controlled by an unseen and heretofore unexplainable power. We have, heretofore, personalized this power and called it God. We have now, however, learned to look upon it as the permeating essence or Principle of all that exists -- the Infinite or Universal Mind.

21. The Universal Mind, being infinite and omnipotent, has unlimited resources at its command, and when we remember that it is also omnipresent, we cannot escape the conclusion that we must be an expression or manifestation of that Mind.

22. A recognition and understanding of the resources of the subconscious mind will indicate that the only difference between the subconscious and the Universal is one of degree. They differ only as a drop of water differs from the ocean. They are the same in kind and quality; the difference is one of degree only.

23. Do you, can you, appreciate the value of this all-important fact; do you realize that a recognition of this tremendous fact places you in touch with Omnipotence? The subconscious mind being the connecting link between the Universal Mind and the conscious mind, is it not evident that the conscious mind can consciously suggest thoughts which the subconscious mind will put into action, and as the subconscious is one with the Universal, is it not evident that no limit can be placed upon its activities?

24. A scientific understanding of this principle will explain the wonderful results which are secured through the power of prayer. The results which are secured in this way are not brought about by any special dispensations of providence, but on the contrary, they are the result of the operation of a perfectly natural law. There is, therefore, nothing either religious or mysterious about it.

25. Yet there are many who are not ready to enter into the discipline necessary to think correctly, even though it is evident that wrong thinking has brought failure.

26. Thought is the only reality; conditions are but the outward manifestations. As the thought changes, all outward or material conditions must change in order to be in harmony with their creator, which is thought.

27. But the thought must be clear cut, steady, fixed, definite, unchangeable. You cannot take one step forward and two steps backward, neither can you spend twenty or thirty years of your life building up negative conditions as the result of negative thoughts, and then expect to see them all melt away as the result of fifteen or twenty minutes of right thinking.

28. If you enter into the discipline necessary to bring about a radical change in your life, you must do so deliberately, after giving the matter careful thought and full consideration, and then you must allow nothing to interfere with your decision.

29. This discipline, this change of thought, this mental attitude, will not only bring you the material things which are necessary for your highest and best welfare, but will bring health and harmonious conditions generally.

30. If you wish harmonious conditions in your life, you must develop a harmonious mental attitude.

31. Your world without will be a reflection of your world within.

32. For your exercise this week, concentrate on Harmony; and when I say concentrate, I mean all that the word implies. Concentrate so deeply, so earnestly, that you will be conscious of nothing but harmony. Remember, we learn by doing. Reading these lessons will get you nowhere. It is in the practical application that the value consists.

"Learn to keep the door shut, keep out of your mind and out of your world, every element that seeks admittance with no definite helpful end in view." - George Mathew Adams

PART FOURTEEN Study Questions with Answers

131. What is the source of all Wisdom, Power and Intelligence? The Universal Mind.

132. Where do all motion, light, heat and color have their origin? In the Universal Energy, which is one manifestation of the Universal Mind.

133. Where does the creative power of thought originate? In the Universal Mind.

134. What is thought? Mind in motion.

135. How is the Universal differentiated in form? The individual is the means by which the Universal produces the various combinations which result in formation of phenomena.

136. How is this accomplished? The power of the individual to think is his ability to act upon the Universal and bring it into manifestation.

137. What is the first form which the Universal takes so far as we know? Electrons, which fill all space.

138. Where do all things have their origin? In mind.

139. What is the result of a change of thought? A change in conditions.

140. What is the result of a harmonious mental attitude? Harmonious conditions in life. Thought, immaterial though it may be, is the matrix that shapes the issues of life.

"The mind has been active in all fields during this fruitful century, but it is to science we must look for the thoughts that have shaped all thinking."

INTRODUCTION - PART FIFTEEN

Experiments with parasites found on plants indicate that even the lowest order of life is enabled to take advantage of natural law. This experiment was made by Jacques Loch, M.D., Ph. D., a member of the Rockefeller Institute.

"In order to obtain the material, potted rose bushes are brought into a room and placed in front of a closed window. If the plants are allowed to dry out, the aphids (parasites), previously wingless, change to winged insects. After the metamorphosis, the animals leave the plants, fly to the window and then creep upward on the glass."

It is evident that these tiny insects found that the plants on which they had been thriving were dead, and that they could therefore secure nothing more to eat and drink from this source. The only method by which they could save themselves from starvation was to grow temporary wings and fly, which they did.

Experiments such as these indicate that Omniscience as well as Omnipotence is omnipresent and that the tiniest living thing can take advantage of it in an emergency.

Part Fifteen will tell you more about the law under which we live. It will explain that these laws operate to our advantage; that all conditions and experiences that come to us are for our benefit; that we gain strength in proportion to the effort expended, and that our happiness is best attained through a conscious cooperation with natural laws.

PART FIFTEEN

1. The laws under which we live are designed solely for our advantage. These laws are immutable and we cannot escape from their operation.

2. All the great eternal forces act in solemn silence, but it is in our power to place ourselves in harmony with them and thus express a life of comparative peace and happiness.

3. Difficulties, inharmonies, and obstacles indicate that we are either refusing to give out what we no longer need, or refusing to accept what we require.

4. Growth is attained through an exchange of the old for the new, of the good for the better. It is a conditional or reciprocal action, for each of us is a complete thought entity and this completeness makes it possible for us to receive only as we give.

5. We cannot obtain what we lack if we tenaciously cling to what we have. We are able to consciously control our conditions as we come to sense the purpose of what we attract, and are able to extract from each experience only what we require for our further growth. Our ability to do this determines the degree of harmony or happiness we attain.

6. The ability to appropriate what we require for our growth continually increases as we reach higher planes and broader visions, and the greater our abilities to know what we require, the more certain we shall be to discern its presence, to attract it and to absorb it. Nothing may reach us except what is necessary for our growth.

7. All conditions and experiences that come to us do so for our benefit. Difficulties and obstacles will continue to come until we absorb their wisdom and gather from them the essentials of further growth.

8. That we reap what we sow is mathematically exact. We gain permanent strength exactly to the extent of the effort required to overcome difficulties.

9. The inexorable requirements of growth demand that we exert the greatest degree of attraction for what is perfectly in accord with us. Our highest happiness will be best attained through our understanding of, and conscious cooperation with natural laws.

10. In order to possess vitality, thought must be impregnated with love. Love is a product of the emotions. It is therefore essential that the emotions be controlled and guided by the intellect and reason.

11. It is love which imparts vitality to thought and thus enables it to germinate. The law of attraction, or the law of love - for they are one and the same, will bring to it the necessary material for its growth and maturity.

12. The first form which thought will find is language, or words. This determines the importance of words; they are the first manifestation of thought -- the vessels in which thought is carried. They take hold of the ether and by setting it in motion reproduce the thought to others in the form of sound.

13. Thought may lead to action of any kind, but whatever the action, it is simply the thought attempting to express itself in visible form. It is evident, therefore, that if we wish desirable conditions, we can afford to entertain only desirable thoughts.

14. This leads to the inevitable conclusion that if we wish to express abundance in our lives, we can afford to think abundance only, and as words are only thoughts taking form, we must be especially careful to use nothing but constructive and harmonious language, which when finally crystallized into objective forms, will prove to our advantage.

15. We cannot escape from the pictures we incessantly photograph on the mind, and this photography of erroneous conceptions is exactly what is being done by the use of words, when we use any form of language which is not identified with our welfare.

16. We manifest more and more life as our thought becomes clarified and takes higher planes. This is obtained with greater facility as we use word pictures that are clearly defined, and relieved of the conceptions attached to them on lower planes of thought.

17. It is with words that we must express our thoughts, and if we are to make use of higher forms of truth, we may use only such material as has been carefully and intelligently selected with this purpose in view.

18. This wonderful power of clothing thoughts in the form of words is what differentiates man from the rest of the animal kingdom. By the use of the written word he has been enabled to look back over the centuries and see the stirring scenes by which he has come into his present inheritance.

19. He has been enabled to come into communion with the greatest writers and thinkers of all time, and the combined record which we possess today is therefore the expression of Universal Thought as it has been seeking to take form in the mind of Man.

20. We know that the Universal Thought has for its goal the creation of form, and we know that the individual thought is likewise forever attempting to express itself in form, and we know that the word is a thought form, and a sentence is a combination of thought forms; therefore, if we wish our ideal to be beautiful or strong, we must see that the words out of which this temple will eventually be created are exact, that they are put together carefully, because accuracy in building words and sentences is the highest form of architecture in civilization and is a passport to success.

21. Words are thoughts and are therefore an invisible and invincible power which will finally objectify themselves in the form they are given.

22. Words may become mental places that will live forever, or they may become shacks which the first breeze will carry away. They may delight the eye as well as the ear; they may contain all knowledge. In them we find the history of the past as well as the hope of the future. They are living messengers from which every human and superhuman activity is born.

23. The beauty of the word consists in the beauty of the thought. The power of the word consists in the power of the thought, and the power of the thought consists in its vitality. How shall we identify a vital thought? What are its distinguishing characteristics? It must have principle. How shall we identify principle?

24. There is a principle of Mathematics, but none of error; there is a principle of health, but none of disease; there is a principle of truth, but none of dishonesty; there is a principle of light, but none of darkness, and there is a principle of abundance, but none of poverty.

25. How shall we know that this is true? Because if we apply the principle of Mathematics correctly we shall be certain of our results. Where there is health there will be no disease. If we know the Truth we cannot be deceived by error. If we let in light there can be no darkness, and where there is abundance there can be no poverty.

26. These are self-evident facts, but the all-important truth that a thought containing principle is vital and therefore contains life and consequently takes root, and eventually but surely and certainly displaces the negative thoughts which by their very nature can contain no vitality, is one which seems to have been overlooked.

27. But this is a fact which will enable you to destroy every manner of discord, lack and limitation.

28. There can be no question but that he who "is wise enough to understand" will readily recognize that the creative power of thought places an invincible weapon in his hands and makes him a master of destiny.

29. In the physical world there is a law of compensation which is that "the appearance of a given amount of energy anywhere means the disappearance of the same amount somewhere else," and so we find that we can get only what we give; if we pledge ourselves to a certain action, we must be prepared to assume the responsibility for the development of that action. The subconscious cannot reason. It takes us at our word. We have asked for something, we are now to receive it; we have made our bed, we are now to lie in it. The die has been cast; the threads will carry out the pattern we have made.

30. For this reason Insight must be exercised so that the thought which we entertain contains no mental, moral or physical germ which we do not wish objectified in our lives.

31. Insight is a faculty of the mind whereby we are enabled to examine facts and conditions at long range, a kind of human telescope. It enables us to understand the difficulties, as well as the possibilities, in any undertaking.

32. Insight enables us to be prepared for the obstacles which we shall meet. We can therefore overcome them before they have any opportunity of causing difficulty.

33. Insight enables us to plan to advantage and turn our thought and attention in the right direction, instead of into channels which can yield no possible return.

34. Insight is therefore absolutely essential for the development of any great achievement, but with it we may enter, explore and possess any mental field.

35. Insight is a product of the world within and is developed in the Silence, by concentration.

36. For your exercise this week, concentrate on Insight. Take your accustomed position and focus the thought on the fact that to have a knowledge of the creative power of thought does not mean to possess the art of thinking. Let the thought dwell on the fact that knowledge does not apply itself; that our actions are not governed by knowledge, but by custom, precedent and habit. That the only way we can get ourselves to apply knowledge is by a determined conscious effort. Call to mind the fact that knowledge unused passes from the mind; that the value of the information is in the application of the principle. Continue this line of thought until you gain sufficient insight to formulate a definite program for applying this principle to your own particular problem.

"Think truly, and thy thoughts

Shall the world's famine feed;

Speak truly, and each word of thine

Shall be a fruitful seed;

Live truly, and thy life shall be

A great and noble creed."

- Horatio Bonar

PART FIFTEEN Study Questions with Answers

141. What determines the degree of harmony which we attain? Our ability to appropriate what we require for our growth from each experience.

142. What do difficulties and obstacles indicate? That they are necessary for our wisdom and spiritual growth.

143. How may these difficulties be avoided? By a conscious understanding of and cooperation with Natural laws.

144. What is the principle by which thought manifests itself in form? The Law of Attraction.

145. How is the necessary material secured by which the growth, development and maturity of the idea take form? The law of love, which is the creative principle of the Universe, imparts vitality to the thought, and the law of attraction brings the necessary substance by the law of growth.

146. How are desirable conditions secured? By entertaining desirable thoughts only.

147. How are undesirable conditions brought about? By thinking, discussing and visualizing conditions of lack, limitation, disease, inharmony and discord of every kind. This mental photography of erroneous conceptions is taken up by the subconscious and the law of attraction will inevitable crystallize it into objective form. That we reap what we sow is scientifically exact.

148. How can we overcome every kind of fear, lack. limitation, poverty and discord? By substituting principle for error.

149. How may we recognize principle? By a conscious realization of the fact that Truth invariably destroys error. We do not have to laboriously shovel the darkness out; all that is necessary is to turn on the light. The same principle applies to every form of negative thought.

150. What is the value of Insight? It enables us to understand the value of making application of the knowledge which we gain. Many seem to think that knowledge will automatically apply itself, which is by no means true.

"To every man there openeth a way,

And the high soul climbs the high way,

And the low soul gropes the low;

And in between on the misty flats,

The rest drift to and fro.

But to every man there openeth

A high way and a low

And every man decideth

The way his soul shall go."

INTRODUCTION - PART SIXTEEN

The vibratory activities of the planetary Universe are governed by a law of periodicity. Everything that lives has periods of birth, growth, fruitage, and decline. These periods are governed by the Septimal Law.

The Law of Sevens governs the days of the week, the phases of the moon, the harmonies of sound, light, heat, electricity, magnetism, atomic structure. It governs the life of individuals and of nations, and it dominates the activities of the commercial world.

Life is growth, and growth is change. Each seven year period takes us into a new cycle. The first seven years is the period of infancy. The next seven, the period of childhood representing the beginning of individual responsibility. The next seven represents the period of adolescence. The fourth period marks the attainment of full growth. The fifth period is the constructive period, when men begin to acquire property, possessions, a home and family. The next, from 35 to 42, is a period of reactions and changes, and this in turn is followed by a period of reconstruction, adjustment and recuperation, so as to be ready for a new cycle of sevens, beginning with the fiftieth year.

Those familiar with these cycles will not be disturbed when things seem to go wrong, but can apply the principles outlined in these lessons with the full assurance that a higher law will invariably control all other laws, and that through an understanding and conscious operation of spiritual laws, we can convert every seeming difficulty into a blessing.

PART SIXTEEN

1. Wealth is a product of labor. Capital is an effect, not a cause; a servant, not a master; a means, not an end.

2. The most commonly accepted definition of wealth is that it consists of all useful and agreeable things which possess exchange value. It is this exchange value which is the predominant characteristic of wealth.

3. When we consider the small addition made by wealth to the happiness of the possessor, we find that the true value consists not in its utility but in its exchange.

4. This exchange value makes it a medium for securing the things of real value whereby our ideals may be realized.

5. Wealth should then never be desired as an end, but simply as a means of accomplishing an end. Success is contingent upon a higher ideal than the mere accumulation of riches, and he who aspires to such success must formulate an ideal for which he is willing to strive.

6. With such an ideal in mind, the ways and means can and will be provided, but the mistake must not be made of substituting the means for the end. There must be a definite fixed purpose, an ideal.

7. Prentice Mulford said: "The man of success is the man possessed of the greatest spiritual understanding, and every great fortune comes of superior and truly spiritual power." Unfortunately, there are those who fail to recognize this power; they forget that Andrew Carnegie's mother had to help support the family when they came to America, that Harriman's father was a poor clergyman with a salary of only $200 a year, that Sir Thomas Lipton started with only 25 cents. These men had no other power to depend upon, but it did not fail them.

8. The power to create depends entirely upon spiritual power. There are three steps: idealization, visualization and materialization. Every captain of industry depends upon this power exclusively. In an article in Everybody's Magazine, Henry M. Flagler, the Standard Oil multi-millionaire, admitted that the secret of his success was his power to see a thing in its completeness. The following conversation with the reporter shows his power of idealization, concentration and visualization, all spiritual powers:

9. "Did you actually vision to yourself the whole thing? I mean, did you, or could you, really close your eyes and see the tracks? And the trains running? And hear the whistles blowing, did you go as far as that?" "Yes." "How clearly?" "Very clearly."

10. Here we have a vision of the law; we see "cause and effect", we see that thought necessarily precedes and determines action. If we are wise, we shall come into a realization of the tremendous fact that no arbitrary condition can exist for a moment, and that human experience is the result of an orderly and harmonious sequence.

11. The successful businessman is more often than not an idealist and is ever striving for higher and higher standards. The subtle forces of thought as they crystallize in our daily moods are what constitute life.

12. Thought is the plastic material with which we build images of our growing conception of life. Use determines its existence. As in all other things, our ability to recognize it and use it properly is the necessary condition for attainment.

13. Premature wealth is but the forerunner of humiliation and disaster, because we cannot permanently retain anything which we do not merit or which we have not earned.

14. The conditions with which we meet in the world without correspond to the conditions which we find in the world within. This is brought about by the law of attraction. How then shall we determine what is to enter into the world within?

15. Whatever enters the mind through the senses or the objective mind will impress the mind and result in a mental image which will become a pattern for the creative energies. These experiences are largely the result of environment, chance, past thinking and other forms of negative thought, and must be subjected to careful analysis before being entertained. On the other hand, we can form our own mental images through our own interior processes of thought regardless of the thoughts of others, regardless of exterior conditions, regardless of environment of every kind, and it is by the exercise of this power that we can control our own destiny, body, mind and soul.

16. It is by the exercise of this power that we take our fate out of the hands of chance, and consciously make for ourselves the experiences which we desire, because when we consciously realize a condition, that condition will eventually manifest in our lives; it is therefore evident that in the last analysis thinking is the one great cause in life.

17. Therefore, to control thought is to control circumstances, conditions, environment, and destiny.

18. How then are we to control thought; what is the process? To think is to create a thought, but the result of the thought will depend upon its form, its quality and its vitality.

19. The form will depend upon the mental images from which it emanates; this will depend upon the depth of the impression, the predominance of the idea, the clarity of the vision, the boldness of the image.

20. The quality depends upon its substance, and this depends upon the material of which the mind is composed. If this material has been woven from thoughts of vigor, strength, courage, determination, the thought will possess these qualities.

21. And finally, the vitality depends upon the feeling with which the thought is impregnated. If the thought is constructive, it will possess vitality; it will have life, it will grow, develop, expand, it will be creative. It will attract to itself everything necessary for its complete development.

22. If the thought is destructive, it will have within itself the germ of its own dissolution; it will die, but in the process of dying, it will bring sickness, disease, and every other form of discord.

23. This we call evil, and when we bring it upon ourselves. Some of us are disposed to attribute our difficulties to a Supreme Being, but this supreme being is simply Mind in equilibrium.

24. It is neither good nor bad, it simply is.

25. Our ability to differentiate it into form is our ability to manifest good or evil.

26. Good and evil therefore are not entities, they are simply words which we use to indicate the result of our actions, and these actions are in turn predetermined by the character of our thought.

27. If our thought is constructive and harmonious we manifest good; if it is destructive and discordant we manifest evil.

28. If you desire to visualize a different environment, the process is simply to hold the ideal in mind until your vision has been made real. Give no thought to persons, places or things; these have no place in the absolute. The environment you desire will contain everything necessary; the right persons and the right things will come at the right time and in the right place.

29. It is sometimes not plain how character, ability, attainment, achievement, environment and destiny can be controlled through the power of visualization, but this is an exact scientific fact.

30. You will readily see that what we think determines the quality of mind, and that the quality of mind in turn determines our ability and mental capacity, and you can readily understand that the improvement in our ability will naturally be followed by increase in attainment and a greater control of circumstances.

31. It will thus be seen that Natural laws work in a perfectly natural and harmonious manner; everything seems to "just happen." If you want any evidence of this fact, simply compare results of your efforts in your own life when your actions were prompted by high ideals, and when you had selfish or ulterior motives in mind. You will need no further evidence. If you wish to bring about the realization of any desire, form a mental picture of success in your mind by consciously visualizing your desire; in this way you will be compelling success, you will be externalizing it in your life by scientific methods.

32. We can only see what already exists in the objective world, but what we visualize already exists in the spiritual world, and this visualization is a substantial token of what will one day appear in the objective world, if we are faithful to our ideal. The reason for this is not difficult. Visualization is a form of imagination. This process of thinking forms impressions on the mind, and these impressions in turn form concepts and ideals, and they in turn are the plans from which the Master architect will weave the future.

33. The psychologists have come to the conclusion that there is but one sense, the sense of feeling, and that all other senses are but modifications of this one sense. This being true, we know why feeling is the very fountainhead of power, why the emotions so easily overcome the intellect, and why we must put feeling into our thought, if we wish results. Thought and feeling is the irresistible combination.

34. Visualization must, of course, be directed by the will. We are to visualize exactly what we want; we must be careful not to let the imagination run riot. Imagination is a good servant but a poor master, and unless it is controlled it may easily lead us into all kinds of speculations and conclusions which have no basis or foundation of fact whatever. Every kind of plausible opinion is liable to be accepted without any analytical examination and the inevitable result is mental chaos.

35. We must therefore construct only such mental images as are known to be scientifically true. Subject every idea to a searching analysis and accept nothing which is not scientifically exact. When you do this you will attempt nothing but what you know you can carry out, and success will crown your efforts. This is what businessmen call far-sightedness; it is much the same as insight, and is one of the great secrets of success in all-important undertakings.

36. For your exercise this week, try to bring yourself to a realization of the important fact that harmony and happiness are states of consciousness and do not depend upon the possession of things; that things are effects and come as a consequence of correct mental states. So that if we desire material possession of any kind, our chief concern should be to acquire the mental attitude which will bring about the result desired. This mental attitude is brought about by a realization of our spiritual nature and our unity with the Universal Mind which is the substance of all things. This realization will bring about everything which is necessary for our complete enjoyment. This is scientific or correct thinking. When we succeed in bringing about this mental attitude, it is comparatively easy to realize our desire as an already accomplished fact. When we can do this we shall have found the "Truth" which makes us "free" from every lack or limitation of any kind.

"A man might frame and let loose a star to roll in its orbit, and yet not have done so memorable a thing before God as he who lets a golden-orbed thought to roll through the generations of time."

- H. W. Beecher

PART SIXTEEN Study Questions with Answers

151. Upon what does wealth depend? Upon an understanding of the creative nature of thought.

152. Upon what does its true value consist? Upon its exchange value.

153. Upon what does success depend? Upon spiritual power.

154. Upon what does this power depend? Upon use; use determines its existence.

155. How may we take our fate out of the hands of chance? By consciously realizing the conditions which we desire to see manifested in our lives.

156. What then is the great business of life? Thinking.

157. Why is this so? Because thought is spiritual and therefore creative. To consciously control thought is therefore to control circumstances, conditions, environment and destiny.

158. What is the source of all evil? Destructive thinking.

159. What is the source of all good? Scientific, correct thinking.

160. What is scientific thinking? A recognition of the creative nature of spiritual energy and our ability to control it.

"The greatest events of an age are its best thoughts. It is the nature of thought to find its way into action."

-Bovee.

INTRODUCTION - PART SEVENTEEN

The kind of Deity which a man consciously or unconsciously worships indicates the intellectual status of the worshipper.

Ask the Indian of God, and he will describe to you a powerful chieftain of a glorious tribe. Ask the Pagan of God, and he will tell you of a God of fire, a God of water, a god of this, that, and the other.

Ask the Israelite of God, and he will tell you of the God of Moses, who conceived it expedient to rule by coercive measures; hence, the Ten Commandments. Or of Joshua, who led the Israelites into battle, confiscated property, murdered the prisoners, and laid waste to cities.

The so-called heathen made "graven images" of their Gods, whom they were accustomed to worship, but among the most intelligent, at least, these images were but the visible fulcrums with which they were enabled to mentally concentrate on the qualities which they desired to externalize in their lives.

We of the twenty-first century worship a God of Love in theory, but in practice we make for ourselves "graven images" of "Wealth," "Power," "Fashion," "Custom" and "Conventionality." We "fall down" before them and worship them. We concentrate on them and they are thereby externalized in our lives.

The student who masters the contents of Part Seventeen will not mistake the symbols for the reality; he will be interested in causes, rather than effects. He will concentrate on the realities of life, and will then not be disappointed in the results.

PART SEVENTEEN

1. We are told that Man has "dominion over all things"; this dominion is established through Mind. Thought is the activity which controls every principle beneath it. The highest principle by reason of its superior essence and qualities necessarily determines the circumstances, aspects and relation of everything with which it comes in contact.

2. The vibrations of Mental forces are the finest and consequently the most powerful in existence. To those who perceive the nature and transcendency of mental force, all physical power sinks into insignificance.

3. We are accustomed to look upon the Universe with a lens of five senses, and from these experiences our anthropomorphic conceptions originate, but true conceptions are only secured by spiritual insight. This insight requires a quickening of the vibrations of the Mind, and is only secured when the mind is continuously concentrated in a given direction.

4. Continuous concentration means an even, unbroken flow of thought and is the result of a patient, persistent, persevering and well-regulated system.

5. Great discoveries are the result of long-continued investigation. The science of mathematics requires years of concentrated effort to master it, and the greatest science -- that of the Mind -- is revealed only through concentrated effort.

6. Concentration is much misunderstood; there seems to be an idea of effort or activity associated with it, when just the contrary is necessary. The greatness of an actor lies in the fact that he forgets himself in the portrayal of his character, becoming so identified with it that the audience is swayed by the realism of the performance. This will give you a good idea of true concentration. You should be so interested in your thought, so engrossed in your subject, as to be conscious of nothing else. Such concentration leads to intuitive perception and immediate insight into the nature of the object concentrated upon.

7. All knowledge is the result of concentration of this kind. It is thus that the secrets of Heaven and Earth have been wrested; it is thus that the mind becomes a magnet and the desire to know draws the knowledge, irresistibly attracts it, makes it your own.

8. Desire is largely subconscious; conscious desire rarely realizes its object when the latter is out of immediate reach. Subconscious desire arouses the latent faculties of the mind, and difficult problems seem to solve themselves.

9. The subconscious mind may be aroused and brought into action in any direction and made to serve us for any purpose, by concentration. The practice of concentration requires the control of the physical, mental, and physical being. All modes of consciousness, whether physical, mental, or physical, must be under control. Spiritual Truth is therefore the controlling factor; it is this which will enable you to grow out of limited attainment and reach a point where you will be able to translate modes of thought into character and consciousness.

10. Concentration does not mean mere thinking of thoughts, but the transmutation of these thoughts into practical values. The average person has no conception of the meaning of concentration. There is always the cry "to have" but never the cry "to be"; they fail to understand that they cannot have one without the other, that they must first find the "kingdom" before they can have the "things added." Momentary enthusiasm is of no value; it is only with unbounded self-confidence that the goal is reached.

11. The mind may place the ideal a little too high and fall short of the mark. It may attempt to soar on untrained wings and instead of flying, fall to earth; but that is no reason for not making another attempt.

12. Weakness is the only barrier to mental attainment. Attribute your weakness to physical limitations or mental uncertainties and try again; ease and perfection are gained by repetition.

13. The astronomer centers his mind on the stars and they give forth their secrets. The geologist centers his mind on the construction of the earth and we have geology; so with all things. Men center their minds on the problems of life, and the result is apparent in the vast and complex social order of the day.

14. All mental discovery and attainment are the result of desire plus concentration. Desire is the strongest mode of action; the more persistent the desire, the more authoritative the revelation. Desire added to concentration will wrench any secret from nature.

15. In realizing great thoughts, in experiencing great emotions that correspond with great thoughts, the mind is in a state where it appreciates the value of higher things.

16. The intensity of one moment's earnest concentration and the intense longing to become and to attain may take you further than years of slow, normal and forced effort. It will unfasten the prison bars of unbelief, weakness, impotence and self-belittlement, and you will come into a realization of the joy of overcoming.

17. The spirit of initiative and originality is developed through persistence and continuity of mental effort. Business teaches the value of concentration and encourages decision of character; it develops practical insight and quickness of conclusion. The mental element in every commercial pursuit is dominant as the controlling factor, and desire is the predominating force. All commercial relations are the externalization of desire.

18. Many of the sturdy and substantial virtues are developed in commercial employment. The mind is steadied and directed; it becomes efficient. The principal necessity is the strengthening of the mind so that it rises superior to the distractions and wayward impulses of instinctive life and thus successfully overcomes in the conflict between the higher and lower self.

19. All of us are dynamos, but the dynamo of itself is nothing. The mind must work the dynamo; then it is useful and its energy can be definitely concentrated. The mind is an engine whose power is undreamed. Thought is an omni-working power. It is the ruler and creator of all form and all events occurring in form. Physical energy is nothing in comparison with the omnipotence of thought, because thought enables man to harness all other natural power.

20. Vibration is the action of thought. It is vibration which reaches out and attracts the material necessary to construct and build. There is nothing mysterious concerning the power of thought; concentration simply implies that consciousness can be focalized to the point where it becomes identified with the object of its attention. As food absorbed is the essence of the body, so the mind absorbs the object of its attention, gives it life and being.

21. If you concentrate on some matter of importance, the intuitive power will be set in operation, and help will come in the nature of information which will lead to success.

22. Intuition arrives at conclusions without the aid of experience or memory. Intuition often solves problems that are beyond the grasp of the reasoning power. Intuition often comes with a suddenness that is startling; it reveals the truth for which we are searching so directly that it seems to come from a higher power. Intuition can be cultivated and developed. In order to do this, it must be recognized and appreciated. If the intuitive visitor is given a royal welcome when he comes, he will come again; the more cordial the welcome the more frequent his visits will become, but if he is ignored or neglected he will make his visits few and far apart.

23. Intuition usually comes in the Silence. Great minds seek solitude frequently; it is here that all the larger problems of life are worked out. For this reason, every businessman who can afford it has a private office where he will not be disturbed. If you cannot afford a private office, you can at least find somewhere where you can be alone a few minutes each day to train the thought along lines which will enable you to develop that invincible power which is necessary to achieve.

24. Remember that fundamentally the subconscious is omnipotent. There is no limit to the things that can be done when it is given the power to act. Your degree of success is determined by the nature of your desire. If the nature of your desire is in harmony with Natural Law or the Universal Mind, it will gradually emancipate the mind and give you invincible courage.

25. Every obstacle conquered, every victory gained, will give you more faith in your power, and you will have greater ability to win. Your strength is determined by your mental attitude. If this attitude is one of success, and is permanently held with an unswerving purpose, you will attract to you from the invisible domain the things you silently demand. By keeping the thought in mind, it will gradually take tangible form. A definite purpose sets causes in motion which go out in the invisible world and find the material necessary to serve your purpose.

26. You may be pursuing the symbols of power instead of power itself. You may be pursuing fame instead of honor, riches instead of wealth, position instead of servitude;

in either event you will find that they turn to ashes just as you overtake them.

27. Premature wealth or position cannot be retained because it has not been earned. We get only what we give, and those who try to get without giving always find that the law of compensation is relentlessly bringing about an exact equilibrium.

28. The race has usually been for money and other mere symbols of power, but with an understanding of the true source of power, we can afford to ignore the symbols. The man with a large bank account finds it unnecessary to load his pockets down with gold; so with the man who has found the true source of power. He is no longer interested in its shams or pretensions.

29. Thought ordinarily leads outwardly in evolutionary directions, but it can be turned within where it will take hold of the basic principles of things, the heart of things, the spirit of things. When you get to the heart of things it is comparatively easy to understand and command them.

30. This is because the Spirit of a thing is the thing itself, the vital part of it, the real substance. The form is simply the outward manifestation of the spiritual activity within.

31. For your exercise this week, concentrate as nearly as possible in accordance with the method outlined in this lesson. Let there be no conscious effort or activity associated with your purpose. Relax completely; avoid any thought of anxiety as to results. Remember that power comes through repose. Let the thought dwell upon your object, until it is completely identified with it, until you are conscious of nothing else.

32. If you wish to eliminate fear, concentrate on courage.

33. If you wish to eliminate lack, concentrate on abundance.

34. If you wish to eliminate disease, concentrate on health.

35. Always concentrate on the ideal as an already existing fact; this is the germ cell, the life principle which goes forth and sets in motion those causes which guide, direct and bring about the necessary relation, which eventually manifest in form.

"Thought is the property of those only who can entertain it." - Emerson

PART SEVENTEEN Study Questions with Answers

161. What is the true method of concentration? To become so identified with the object of your thought that you are conscious of nothing else.

162. What is the result of this method of concentration? Invisible forces are set in motion which irresistibly bring about conditions in correspondence with your thought.

163. What is the controlling factor in this method of thought? Spiritual Truth.

164. Why is this so? Because the nature of our desire must be in harmony with Natural Law.

165. What is the practical value of this method of concentration? Thought is transmuted into character, and character is the magnet which creates the environment of the individual.

166. What is the controlling factor in every commercial pursuit? The mental element.

167. Why is this so? Because Mind is the ruler and creator of all form and all events occurring in form.

168. How does concentration operate? By the development of the powers of perception, wisdom, intuition, and sagacity.

169. Why is intuition superior to reason? Because it does not depend upon experience or memory, and frequently brings about the solution to our problems by methods concerning which we are in entire ignorance.

170. What is the result of pursuing the symbol of the reality? They frequently turn to ashes just as we overtake them, because the symbol is only the outward form of the spiritual activity within; therefore unless we can possess the spiritual reality, the form disappears.

INTRODUCTION - PART EIGHTEEN

In order to grow we must obtain what is necessary for our growth. This is brought about through the law of attraction. This principle is the sole means by which the individual is differentiated from the Universal.

Think for a moment, what would a man be if he were not a husband, father, or brother, if he were not interested in the social, economical, political or religious world. He would be nothing but an abstract theoretical ego. He exists, therefore, only in his relation to the whole, in his relation to other men, in his relation to society. This relation constitutes his environment and in no other way.

It is evident, therefore, that the individual is simply the differentiation of the one Universal Mind "which lighteth every man that cometh into the world," and his so-called individuality or personality consists of nothing but the manner in which he relates with the whole.

This we call his environment and is brought about by the law of attraction. Part Eighteen, which follows, has something more to say concerning this important law.

PART EIGHTEEN

1. There is a change in the thought of the world. This change is silently transpiring in our midst, and is more important than any which the world has undergone since the downfall of Paganism.

2. The present revolution in the opinions of all classes of men, the highest and most cultured of men as well as those of the laboring class, stands unparalleled in the history of the world.

3. Science has of late made such vast discoveries, has revealed such an infinity of resources, has unveiled such enormous possibilities and such unsuspected forces, that scientific men more and more hesitate to affirm certain theories as established and beyond doubt, or to deny other theories as absurd or impossible.

4. A new civilization is being born. Customs, creeds, and precedent are passing; vision, faith and service are taking their place. The fetters of tradition are being melted off from humanity, and as the impurities of materialism are being consumed, thought is being liberated and truth is rising full robed before an astonished multitude.

5. The whole world is on the eve of a new consciousness, a new power, and a new realization within the self.

6. Physical Science has resolved matter into molecules, molecules into atoms, atoms into energy, and it has remained for Mr. J. A. Fleming, in an address before the Royal Institution, to resolve this energy into mind. He says, "In its ultimate essence, energy may be incomprehensible by us except as an exhibition of the direct operation of that which we call Mind or Will."

7. And this mind is the indwelling and ultimate. It is imminent in matter as in spirit. It is the sustaining, energizing, all-pervading Spirit of the universe.

8. Every living thing must be sustained by this omnipotent Intelligence, and we find the difference in individual lives to be largely measured by the degree of this intelligence which they manifest. It is greater intelligence that places the animal in a higher scale of being than the plant, the man higher than the animal, and we find that this increased intelligence is again indicated by the power of the individual to control modes of action and thus to consciously adjust himself to his environment.

9. It is this adjustment that occupies the attention of the greatest minds, and this adjustment consists in nothing else than the recognition of an existing order in the universal mind, for it is well known that this mind will obey us precisely in proportion as we first obey it.

10. It is the recognition of Natural Laws that has enabled us to annihilate time and space, to soar in the air and to make iron float, and the greater the degree of intelligence, the greater will be our recognition of these Natural Laws and the greater will be the power we can possess.

11. It is the recognition of the self as an individualization of this Universal Intelligence that enables the individual to control those forms of intelligence which have not yet reached this level of self-recognition; they do not know that this Universal Intelligence permeates all things ready to be called into action. They do not know that it is responsive to every demand, and they are therefore in bondage to the law of their own being.

12. Thought is creative and the principle on which the law is based is sound and legitimate and is inherent in the nature of things; but this creative power does not originate in the individual, but in the universal, which is the source and foundation of all energy and substance. The individual is simply the channel for the distribution of this energy.

13. The individual is simply the means by which the universal produces the various combinations which result in the formation of phenomena, which depends upon the law of vibration whereby various rates of rapidity of motion in the primary substance form new substances only in certain exact numerical ratios.

14. Thought is the invisible link by which the individual comes into communication with the Universal, the finite with the Infinite, the seen with the Unseen. Thought is the magic by which the human is transformed into a being who thinks and knows and feels and acts.

15. As the proper apparatus has enabled the eye to discover worlds without, number millions of miles away, so with the proper understanding man has been enabled to communicate with the Universal Mind, the source of all power.

16. The Understanding which is usually developed is about as valuable as a VCR without a videotape; in fact, it is usually nothing more than a "belief", which means nothing at all. The savages of the Cannibal Islands believe something, but that proves nothing.

17. The only belief which is of any value to anyone is a belief that has been put to a test and demonstrated to be a fact. It is then no longer a belief, but has become a living Faith or Truth.

18. And this Truth has been put to the test by hundreds of thousands of people and has been found to be the Truth exactly in proportion to the usefulness of the apparatus which they used.

19. A man would not expect to locate stars hundreds of millions of miles away without a sufficiently strong telescope, and for this reason Science is continually engaged in building larger and more powerful telescopes and is continually rewarded by additional knowledge of the heavenly bodies.

20. So with understanding; men are continually making progress in the methods which they use to come into communication with the Universal Mind and its infinite possibilities.

21. The Universal Mind manifests itself in the objective, through the principle of attraction that each atom has for every other atom, in infinite degrees of intensity.

22. It is by this principle of combining and attracting that things are brought together. This principle is of universal application and is the sole means whereby the purpose of existence is carried into effect.

23. The expression of growth is met in a most beautiful manner through the instrumentality of this Universal Principle.

24. In order to grow we must obtain what is essential for our growth, but as we are at all times a complete thought entity, this completeness makes it possible for us to receive only as we give. Growth is therefore conditioned on reciprocal action, and we find that on the mental plane like attracts like, that mental vibrations respond only to the extent of their vibratory harmony.

25. It is clear, therefore, that thoughts of abundance will respond only to similar thoughts; the wealth of the individual is seen to be what he inherently is. Affluence within is found to be the secret of attraction for affluence without. The ability to produce is found to be the real source of wealth of the individual. It is for this reason that he who has his heart in his work is certain to meet with unbounded success. He will give and continually give, and the more he gives, the more he will receive.

26. What do the great financiers of Wall Street, the captains of industry, the statesmen, the great corporation attorneys, the inventors, the physicians, the authors -- what do each of these contribute to the sum of human happiness but the power of their thought?

27. Thought is the energy by which the law of attraction is brought into operation, which eventually manifests in abundance.

28. The Universal Mind is Static Mind or Substance in equilibrium. It is differentiated into form by our power to think. Thought is the dynamic phase of mind.

29. Power depends upon consciousness of power. Unless we use it, we shall lose it, and unless we are conscious of it, we cannot use it.

30. The use of this power depends upon attention; the degree of attention determines our capacity for the acquirement of knowledge which is another name for power.

31. Attention has been held to be the distinguishing mark of genius. The cultivation of attention depends upon practice.

32. The incentive of attention is interest. The greater the interest, the greater the attention. The greater the attention, the greater the interest, action and reaction. Begin by paying attention; before long you will have aroused interest. This interest will attract more attention, and this attention will produce more interest, and so on. This practice will enable you to cultivate the power of attention.

33. This week, concentrate upon your power to create. Seek insight, perception. Try to find a logical basis for the faith which is in you. Let the thought dwell on the fact that the physical man lives and moves and has his being in the sustainer of all organic life, air that he must breathe to live. Then let the thought rest on the fact that the spiritual man also lives and moves and has his being in a similar, but subtler energy upon which he must depend for life, and that as in the physical world no life assumes form until after a seed is sown, and no higher fruit than that of the parent stock can be produced, so in the spiritual world no effect can be produced until the seed is sown, and the fruit will depend upon the nature of the seed, so that the results which you secure depend upon your perception of law in the mighty domain of causation, the highest evolution of human consciousness.

"There is no thought in my mind but it quickly tends to convert itself into a power and organizes a huge instrumentality of means." - Emerson

PART EIGHTEEN Study Questions with Answers

171. How is the difference in individual lives measured? By the degree of intelligence which they manifest.

172. What is the law by which the individual may control other forms of intelligence? A recognition of the self as an individualization of the Universal Intelligence.

173. Where does the creative power originate? In the Universal.

174. How does the Universal create form? By means of the individual.

175. What is the connecting link between the individual and the Universal? Thought.

176. What is the principle by which the means of existence is carried into effect? The Law of Love.

177. How is this principle brought into expression? By the Law of Growth.

178. Upon what condition does the law of growth depend? Upon reciprocal action. The individual is complete at all times and this makes it possible to receive only as we give.

179. What is it that we give? Thought.

180. What do we receive? Thought, which is substance in equilibrium and which is constantly being differentiated in form by what we think.

INTRODUCTION - PART NINETEEN

Fear is a powerful form of thought. It paralyzes the nerve centers, thus affecting the circulation of the blood. This, in turn, paralyzes the muscular system, so that fear affects the entire being, body, brain and nerve, physical, mental, and muscular.

Of course the way to overcome fear is to become conscious of power. What is this mysterious vital force which we call power? We do not know, but then, neither do we know what electricity is. But we do know that by conforming to the requirements of the law by which electricity is governed, it will be our obedient servant; that it will light our homes, our cities, run our machinery, and serve us in many useful capacities.

And so it is with vital force. Although we do not know what it is, and possibly may never know, we do know that it is a primary force which manifests through living bodies, and that by complying with the laws and principles by which it is governed, we can open ourselves to a more abundant inflow of this vital energy, and thus express the highest possible degree of mental, moral, and spiritual efficiency.

This part tells of a very simple way of developing this vital force. If you put into practice the information outlined in this lesson, you will soon develop the sense of power which has ever been the distinguishing mark of genius.

PART NINETEEN

1. The search for truth is no longer a haphazard adventure, but it is a systematic process, and is logical in its operation. Every kind of experience is given a voice in shaping its decision.

2. In seeking the truth we are seeking ultimate cause. We know that every human experience is an effect. Then, if we may ascertain the cause, and if we shall find that this cause is one which we can consciously control, the effect or the experience will be within our control also.

3. Human experience will then no longer be the football of fate. A man will not be the child of fortune, but destiny. Fate and fortune will be controlled as readily as a captain controls his ship, or an engineer his train.

4. All things are finally resolvable into the same element, and as they are thus translatable one into the other, they must ever be in relation and may never be in opposition to one another.

5. In the physical world there are innumerable contrasts, and these may for convenience sake be designated by distinctive names. There are sizes, colors, shades or ends to all things. There is a North Pole, and a South Pole, an inside and an outside, a seen and an unseen, but these expressions merely serve to place extremes in contrast.

6. They are names given to two different parts of one quantity. The two extremes are relative; they are not separate entities, but are two parts or aspects of the whole.

7. In the mental world we find the same law. We speak of knowledge and ignorance, but ignorance is but a lack of knowledge and is therefore found to be simply a word to express the absence of knowledge; it has no principle in itself.

8. In the Moral World we again find the same law. We speak of good and evil, but Good is a reality, something tangible, while Evil is found to be simply a negative condition, the absence of Good. Evil is sometimes thought to be a very real condition, but it has no principle, no vitality, no life. We know this because it can always be destroyed by Good. Just as Truth destroys Error and light destroys darkness, so Evil vanishes when Good appears; there is therefore but one principle in the Moral World.

9. We find exactly the same law obtaining in the Spiritual world. We speak of Mind and Matter as two separate entities, but clearer insight makes it evident that there is but one operative principle and that is Mind.

10. Mind is the real and the eternal. Matter is forever changing; we know that in the eons of time, a hundred years is but as a day. If we stand in any large city and let the eye rest on the innumerable large and magnificent buildings, the vast array of modern automobiles, cellular telephones, the electric lights, and all the other conveniences of modern civilization, we may remember that not one of them was there just over a century ago, and if we could stand on the same spot in a hundred years from now, in all probability we should find that but few of them remained.

11. In the animal kingdom we find the same law of change. The millions and millions of animals come and go, a few years constituting their span of life. In the plant world the change is still more rapid. Many plants and nearly all grasses come and go in a single year. When we pass to the inorganic, we expect to find something more substantial, but as we gaze on the apparently solid continent, we are told that it arose from the ocean; we see the giant mountain and are told that the place where it now stands was once a lake; and as we stand in awe before the great cliffs in the Yosemite Valley we can easily trace the path of the glaciers which carried all before them.

12. We are in the presence of continual change, and we know that this change is but the evolution of the Universal Mind, the grand process whereby all things are continually being created anew, and we come to know that matter is but a form which Mind takes and is therefore simply a condition. Matter has no principle; Mind is the only principle.

13. We have then come to know that Mind is the only principle which is operative in the physical, mental, moral and spiritual world.

14. We also know that this mind is static, mind at rest. We also know that the ability of the individual to think is his ability to act upon the Universal Mind and convert it into dynamic mind, or mind in motion.

15. In order to do this, fuel must be applied in the form of food, for man cannot think without eating, and so we find that even a spiritual activity such as thinking cannot be converted into sources of pleasure and profit except by making use of material means.

16. It requires energy of some kind to collect electricity and convert it into a dynamic power. It requires the rays of the sun to give the necessary energy to sustain plant life. So it also requires energy in the form of food to enable the individual to think and thereby act upon the Universal Mind.

17. You may know that thought constantly, eternally is taking form, is forever seeking expression, or you may not; but the fact remains that if your thought is powerful, constructive, and positive, this will be plainly evident in the state of your health, your business and your environment. If your thought is weak, critical, destructive and negative generally, it will manifest in your body as fear, worry and nervousness, in your finance as lack and limitation, and in discordant conditions in your environment.

18. All wealth is the offspring of power. Possessions are of value only as they confer power. Events are significant only as they affect power. All things represent certain forms and degrees of power.

19. A knowledge of cause and effect as shown by the laws governing steam, electricity, chemical affinity and gravitation enables men to plan courageously and to execute fearlessly. These laws are called Natural Laws, because they govern the physical world, but all power is not physical power; there is also mental power, and there is moral and spiritual power.

20. What are our schools, our universities, but mental powerhouses, places where mental power is being developed?

21. As there are many mighty powerhouses for the application of power to ponderous machinery, whereby raw material is collected and converted into the necessities and comforts of life, so the mental powerhouses collect the raw material and cultivate and develop it into a power which is infinitely superior to all the forces of nature, marvelous though they may be.

22. What is this raw material which is being collected in these thousands of mental powerhouses all over the world and developed into a power which is evidently controlling every other power? In its static form it is Mind - in its dynamic form, it is Thought.

23. This power is superior because it exists on a higher plane, because it has enabled man to discover the law by which these wonderful forces of Nature could be harnessed and made to do the work of hundreds and thousands of men. It has enabled man to discover laws whereby time and space have been annihilated, and the law of gravitation overcome.

24. Thought is the vital force or energy which is being developed and which has produced such startling results in the last half century as to bring about a world which would be absolutely inconceivable to a man existing only 50 or 25 years ago. If such results have been secured by organizing these mental powerhouses in 50 years, what may not be expected in another 50 years?

25. The substance from which all things are created is infinite in quantity. We know that light travels at the rate of 186,000 miles per second, and we know that there are stars so remote that it takes light 2,000 years to reach us, and we know that such starts exist in all parts of the heaven; we know, too, that this light comes in waves, so that if the ether on which these waves travel was not continuous the light would fail to reach us. We can then only come to the conclusion that this substance, or ether, or raw material, is universally present.

26. How, then, does it manifest in form? In electrical science, a battery is formed by connecting the opposite poles of zinc and copper, which causes a current to flow from one to the other and so provides energy. This same process is repeated in respect to every polarity, and as all form simply depends upon the rate of vibration and consequent relations of atoms to each other, if we wish to change the form of manifestation we must change the polarity. This is the principle of causation.

27. For your exercise this week, concentrate, and when I use the word concentrate, I mean all that the word implies. Become so absorbed in the object of your thought that you are conscious of nothing else, and do this a few minutes every day. You take the necessary time to eat in order that the body may be nourished, why not take the time to assimilate your mental food?

28. Let the thought rest on the fact that appearances are deceptive. The earth is not flat, neither is it stationary; the sky is not a dome, the sun does not move, the stars are not small specks of light, and matter which was once supposed to be fixed has been found to be in a state of perpetual flux.

29. Try to realize that the day is fast approaching -- its dawn is now at hand -- when modes of thought and action must be adjusted to rapidly increasing knowledge of the operation of eternal principles.

"Silent thought, is, after all, the mightiest agent in human affairs." - Channing

PART NINETEEN Study Questions with Answers

181. How are extremes placed in contrast? They are designated by distinctive names, such as inside and outside, top and bottom, light and dark, good and bad.

182. Are these separate entities? No, they are parts or aspects of one Whole.

183. What is the one creative Principle in the physical, mental and spiritual world? The Universal Mind, or the Eternal Energy from which all things proceed.

184. How are we related to this creative Principle? By our ability to think.

185. How does this creative Principle become operative? Thought is the seed which results in action and action results in form.

186. Upon what does form depend? Upon the rate of vibration.

187. How may the rate of vibration be changed? By mental action.

188. Upon what does mental action depend? Upon polarity, action and reaction, between the individual and the Universal.

189. Does the creative energy originate in the individual or the Universal? In the Universal, but the Universal can manifest only through the individual.

190. Why is the individual necessary? Because the Universal is static and requires energy to start it in motion. This is furnished by food which is converted into energy, which in turn enables the individual to think. When the individual stops eating he stops thinking; then he no longer acts upon the Universal. There is consequently no longer any action or reaction, the Universal is then only pure mind in static form -- mind at rest.

INTRODUCTION - PART TWENTY

For many years there has been an endless discussion as to the origin of evil. Theologians have told us that God is Love, and that God is Omnipresent. If this be true, there is no place where God is not. Where, then, is Evil, Satan and Hell? Let us see:

God is Spirit.

Spirit is the Creative Principle of the Universe.

Man is made in the image and likeness of God.

Man is therefore a spiritual being.

The only activity which spirit possesses is the power to think.

Thinking is therefore a creative process.

All form is therefore the result of the thinking process.

The destruction of form must also be a result of the thinking process.

Fictitious representations of form are the result of the creative power of thought, as in Hypnotism.

Apparent representations of form are the result of the creative power of thought, as in Spiritualism.

Invention, organization and constructive work of all kinds are the result of the creative power of thought, as in concentration.

When the creative power of thought is manifested for the benefit of humanity, we call the result good.

When the creative power of thought is manifested in a destructive or evil manner, we call the result evil.

This indicates the origin of both good and evil; they are simply words which have been coined in order to indicate the nature of the result of the thinking or creative process.

Thought necessarily precedes and predetermines action; action precedes and predetermines condition.

Part Twenty will throw more light upon this important subject.

PART TWENTY

1. The spirit of a thing is that thing; it is necessarily fixed, changeless and eternal. The spirit of you is -- you; without the spirit you would be nothing. It becomes active through your recognition of it and its possibilities.

2. You may have all the wealth in Christendom, but unless you recognize it and make use of it, it will have no value. So with your spiritual wealth: unless you recognize it and use it, it will have no value. The one and only condition of spiritual power is use or recognition.

3. All great things come through recognition. The scepter of power is consciousness and thought is its messenger, and this messenger is constantly molding the realities of the invisible world into the conditions and environments of your objective world.

4. Thinking is the true business of life; power is the result. You are at all times dealing with the magical power of thought and consciousness. What results can you expect so long as you remain oblivious to the power which has been placed within your control?

5. So long as you do this, you limit yourself to superficial conditions and make of yourself a beast of burden for those who think, those who recognize their power, those who know that unless we are willing to think we shall have to work, and the less we think the more we shall have to work, and the less we shall get for our work.

6. The secret of power is a perfect understanding of the principles, forces, methods and combinations of Mind and a perfect understanding of our relationship to the Universal Mind. It is well to remember that this principle is unchangeable; if this were not so, it would not be reliable. All principles are changeless.

7. This stability is your opportunity; you are its active attribute, the channel for its activity. The Universal can act only through the individual.

8. When you begin to perceive that the essence of the Universal is within yourself -- is you -- you begin to do things, you begin to feel your power. It is the fuel which fires the imagination, which lights the torch of inspiration, which gives vitality to thought, which enables you to connect with all the invisible forces of the Universe. It is this power which will enable you to plan fearlessly, to execute masterfully.

9. But perception will come only in the Silence; this seems to be the condition required for all great purposes. You are a visualizing entity. Imagination is your workshop. It is here that your ideal is to be visualized.

10. As a perfect understanding of the nature of this power is a primary condition for its manifestation, visualize the entire method over and over again, so that you may use it whenever occasion requires. The infinity of wisdom is to follow the method whereby we may have the inspiration of the omnipotent Universal Mind on demand at any time.

11. We can fail to recognize this world within, and so exclude it from our consciousness, but it will still be the basic fact of all existence; and when we learn to recognize it, not only in ourselves but in all persons, events, things and circumstances, we shall have found the "Kingdom of heaven" which we are told is "within" us.

12. Our failures are a result of the operation of exactly the same principle. The principle is unchangeable. Its operation is exact; there is no deviation. If we think lack, limitation, discord, we shall find their fruits on every hand; if we think poverty, unhappiness or disease, the thought messengers will carry the summons as readily as any other kind of thought and the result will be just as certain. If we fear a coming calamity, we shall be able to say with Job, "the thing I feared has come upon me"; if we think unkindly or ignorantly we shall thus attract to ourselves the results of our ignorance.

13. This power of thought, if understood and correctly used, is the greatest labor-saving device ever dreamed of, but if not understood or improperly used, the result will in all probability be disastrous, as we have already seen. By the help of this power you can confidently undertake things that are seemingly impossible, because this power is the secret of all inspiration, all genius.

14. To become inspired means to get out of the beaten path, out of the rut, because extraordinary results require extraordinary means. When we come into a recognition of the Unity of all things and that the source of all power is within, we tap the source of inspiration.

15. Inspiration is the art of imbibing; the art of self-realization; the art of adjusting the individual mind to that of the Universal Mind; the art of attaching the proper mechanism to the source of all power; the art of differentiating the formless into form; the art of becoming a channel for the flow of Infinite Wisdom; the art of visualizing perfection; the art of realizing the omnipresence of Omnipotence.

16. An understanding and appreciation of the fact that the infinite power is omnipresent and is therefore in the infinitely small as well as the infinitely large will enable us to absorb its essence. A further understanding of the fact that this power is spirit and therefore indivisible will enable us to appreciate its present at all points at the same time.

17. An understanding of these facts, first intellectually and then emotionally, will enable us to drink deeply from this ocean of infinite power. An intellectual understanding will be of no assistance; the emotions must be brought into action. Thought without feeling is cold. The required combination is thought and feeling.

18. Inspiration is from within. The Silence is necessary, the senses must be stilled, the muscles relaxed, repose cultivated. When you have thus come into possession of a sense of poise and power you will be ready to receive the information or inspiration or wisdom which may be necessary for the development of your purpose.

19. Do not confuse these methods with those of the clairvoyant; they have nothing in common. Inspiration is the art of receiving and makes for all that is best in life. Your business in life is to understand and command these invisible forces instead of letting them command and rule you. Power implies service; inspiration implies power; to understand and apply the method of inspiration is to become a superman.

20. We can live more abundantly every time we breathe, if we consciously breathe with that intention. The IF is a very important condition in this case, as the intention governs the attention, and without the attention you can secure only the results which every one else secures. That is, a supply equal to the demand.

21. In order to secure the larger supply, your demand must be increased, and as you consciously increase the demand the supply will follow; you will find yourself coming into a larger and larger supply of life, energy and vitality.

22. The reason for this is not difficult to understand, but it is another of the vital mysteries of life which does not seem to be generally appreciated. If you make it your own, you will find it one of the great realities of life.

23. We are told that "In Him we live and move and have our being," and we are told that "He" is a Spirit, and again that "He" is Love, so that every time we breathe, we breathe this life, love, and spirit. This is Pranic Energy, or Pranic Ether, we could not exist a moment without it. It is the Cosmic Energy; it is the Life of the Solar Plexus.

24. Every time we breathe we fill our lungs with air and at the same time vitalize our body with this Pranic Ether which is Life itself, so that we have the opportunity of making a conscious connection with All Life, All Intelligence and All Substance.

25. A knowledge of your relation and oneness with this Principle that governs the Universe, and the simple method whereby you can consciously identify yourself with it, gives you a scientific understanding of a law whereby you may free yourself from disease, from lack or limitation of any kind; in fact, it enables you to breathe the "breath of life" into your own nostrils.

26. This "breath of life" is a super-conscious reality. It is the essence of the "I am." It is pure "Being" or Universal Substance, and our conscious unity with it enables us to localize it, and thus exercise the powers of this creative energy.

27. Thought is creative vibration, and the quality of the conditions created will depend upon the quality of our thought, because we cannot express powers which we do not possess. We must "be" before we can "do" and we can "do" only to the extent to which we "are," and so what we do will necessarily coincide with what we "are" and what we are depends upon what we "think." Every time you think, you start a train of causation which will create a condition in strict accordance with the quality of the thought which originated it. Thought which is in harmony with the Universal Mind will result in corresponding conditions. Thought which is destructive or discordant will produce corresponding results. You may use thought constructively or destructively, but the immutable law will not allow you to plant a thought of one kind and reap the fruit of another. You are free to use this marvelous creative power as you will, but you must take the consequences.

28. This is the danger from what is called Will Power. There are those who seem to think that by force of will they can coerce this law; that they can sow seed of one kind and by "Will Power" make it bear fruit of another, but the fundamental principle of creative power is in the Universal, and therefore the idea of forcing a compliance with our wishes by the power of the individual will is an inverted conception which may appear to succeed for a while but is eventually doomed to failure - because it antagonizes the very power which it is seeking to use.

29. It is the individual attempting to coerce the Universal, the finite in conflict with the Infinite. Our permanent well-being will be best conserved by a conscious cooperation with the continuous forward movement of the Great Whole.

30. For your exercise this week, go into the Silence and concentrate on the fact that "In him we live and move and have our being" is literally and scientifically exact! That you ARE because He IS, that if He is Omnipresent He must be in you. That if He is all in all you must be in Him! That He is Spirit and you are made in "His image and likeness" and that the only difference between His spirit and your spirit is one of degree, that a part must be the same in kind and quality as the whole. When you can realize this clearly you will have found the secret of the creative power of thought; you will have found the origin of both good and evil; you will have found the secret of the wonderful power of concentration; you will have found the key to the solution of every problem, whether physical, financial, or environmental.

"The power to think consecutively and deeply and clearly, is an avowed and deadly enemy to mistakes and blunders, superstitions, unscientific theories, irrational beliefs, unbridled enthusiasm, fanaticism."

–   Haddock

PART TWENTY Study Questions with Answers

191. Upon what condition does power depend? Upon recognition and use.

192. What is recognition? Consciousness.

193. How do we become conscious of power? By thinking.

194. What then is the true business of life? Correct scientific thinking.

195. What is correct scientific thinking? The ability to adjust our thought processes to the will of the Universal. In other words, to cooperate with Natural laws.

196. How is this accomplished? By securing a perfect understanding of the principles, forces, methods and combinations of mind.

197. What is this Universal Mind? The basic fact of all existence.

198. What is the cause of all lack, limitation, disease and discord? It is due to the operation of exactly the same law, the law operates relentlessly and is continually bringing about conditions in correspondence with the thought which originated or created them.

199. What is inspiration? The art of realizing the omnipresence of Omniscience.

200. Upon what does the conditions with which we meet depend? Upon the quality of our thought. Because what we do depends upon what we are and what we are depends upon what we think.

INTRODUCTION - PART TWENTY-ONE

It is my privilege to enclose Part Twenty-One. In paragraph 7 you will find that one of the secrets of success, one of the methods of organizing victory, one of the accomplishments of the Master Mind is to think big thoughts.

In paragraph 8 you will find that everything which we hold in our consciousness for any length of time becomes impressed upon our subconsciousness and so becomes a pattern which the creative energy will wave into our life and environment. This is the secret of the wonderful power of prayer.

We know that the universe is governed by law; that for every effect there must be a cause, and that the same cause, under the same conditions, will invariably produce the same effect. Consequently, if prayer has ever been answered, it will always be answered if the proper conditions are complied with. This must necessarily be true, otherwise the universe would be a chaos instead of a cosmos. The answer to prayer is therefore subject to law, and this law is definite, exact and scientific, just as are the laws governing gravitation and electricity. An understanding of this law takes the foundation of Christianity out of the realm of superstition and credulity and places it upon the firm rock of scientific understanding.

But, unfortunately, there are comparatively few persons who know how to pray. They understand that there are laws governing electricity, mathematics, and chemistry, but for some inexplicable reason, it never seems to occur to them that there are also spiritual laws, and that these laws are also definite, scientific, exact, and operate with immutable precision.

PART TWENTY-ONE

1. The real secret of power is consciousness of power. The Universal Mind is unconditional; therefore, the more conscious we become of our unity with this mind, the less conscious we shall become of conditions and limitations, and as we become emancipated or freed from conditions we come into a realization of the unconditional. We have become free!

2. As soon as we become conscious of the inexhaustible power in the world within, we begin to draw on this power and apply and develop the greater possibilities which this discernment has realized, because whatever we become conscious of is invariably manifested in the objective world, is brought forth into tangible expression.

3. This is because the Infinite mind, which is the source from which all things proceed, is one and indivisible, and each individual is a channel whereby this Eternal Energy is being manifested. Our ability to think is our ability to act upon this Universal substance, and what we think is what is created or produced in the objective world.

4. The result of this discovery is nothing less than marvelous, and means that mind is extraordinary in quality, limitless in quantity, and contains possibilities without number. To become conscious of this power is to become a "live wire"; it has the same effect as placing an ordinary wire in contact with a wire that is charged. The Universal is the live wire. It carries power sufficient to meet every situation which may arise in the life of every individual. When the individual mind touches the Universal Mind it receives all the power it requires. This is the world within. All science recognizes the reality of this world, and all power is contingent upon our recognition of this world.

5. The ability to eliminate imperfect conditions depends upon mental action, and mental action depends upon consciousness of power; therefore, the more conscious we become of our unity with the source of all power, the greater will be our power to control and master every condition.

6. Large ideas have a tendency to eliminate all smaller ideas so that it is well to hold ideas large enough to counteract and destroy all small or undesirable tendencies. This will remove innumerable petty and annoying obstacles from your path. You also become conscious of a larger world of thought, thereby increasing your mental capacity as well as placing yourself in position to accomplish something of value.

7. This is one of the secrets of success, one of the methods of organizing victory, one of the accomplishments of the Mastermind. He thinks big thoughts. The creative energies of mind find no more difficulty in handling large situations than small ones. Mind is just as much present in the Infinitely large as in the Infinitely small.

8. When we realize these facts concerning mind, we understand how we may bring ourselves any condition by creating the corresponding conditions in our consciousness, because everything which is held for any length of time in the consciousness eventually becomes impressed upon the subconscious and thus becomes a pattern which the creative energy will wave into the life and environment of the individual.

9. In this way conditions are produced and we find that our lives are simply the reflection of our predominant thoughts, our mental attitude. We see then that the science of correct thinking is the one science, that it includes all other sciences.

10. From this science we learn that every thought creates an impression on the brain, that these impressions create mental tendencies, and these tendencies create character, ability and purpose, and that the combined action of character, ability and purpose determines the experiences with which we shall meet in life.

11. These experiences come to us through the law of attraction; through the action of this law we meet in the world without, the experiences which correspond to our world within.

12. The predominant thought or the mental attitude is the magnet, and the law is that "like attracts like", consequently the mental attitude will invariably attract such conditions as correspond to its nature.

13. This mental attitude is our personality and is composed of the thoughts which we have been creating in our own mind; therefore, if we wish a change in conditions all that is necessary is to change our thought. This will in turn change our mental attitude, which will in turn change our personality, which will in turn change the persons, things and conditions, or the experiences with which we meet in life.

14. It is, however, no easy matter to change the mental attitude, but by persistent effort it may be accomplished. The mental attitude is patterned after the mental pictures which have been photographed on the brain; if you do not like the pictures, destroy the negatives and create new pictures. This is the art of visualization.

15. As soon as you have done this you will begin to attract new things, and the new things will correspond to the new pictures. To do this, impress on the mind a perfect picture of the desire which you wish to have objectified and continue to hold the picture in mind until results are obtained.

16. If the desire is one which requires determination, ability, talent, courage, power or any other spiritual power, these are necessary essentials for your picture; build them in, they are the vital part of the picture. They are the feeling which combines with thought and creates the irresistible magnetic power which draws the things you require to you. They give your picture life, and life means growth, and as soon as it beings to grow, the result is practically assured.

17. Do not hesitate to aspire to the highest possible attainments in anything you may undertake, for the mind forces are ever ready to lend themselves to a purposeful will in the effort to crystallize its highest aspirations into acts, accomplishments, and events. An illustration of how these mind forces operate is suggested by the method in which all our habits are formed. We do a thing, then do it again, and again, and again, until it becomes easy and perhaps almost automatic; and the same rule applies in breaking any and all bad habits. We stop doing a thing, and then avoid it again and again until we are entirely free from it. And if we do fail now and then, we should by no means lose hope, for the law is absolute and invincible and gives us credit for every effort and every success, even though our efforts and successes are perhaps intermittent.

18. There is no limit to what this law can do for you. Dare to believe in your own idea. Remember that Nature is plastic to the ideal. Think of the ideal as an already accomplished fact.

19. The real battle of life is one of ideas. It is being fought out by the few against the many. On the one side is the constructive and creative thought, on the other side the destructive and negative thought. The creative thought is dominated by an ideal, the passive thought is dominated by appearances. On both sides are men of science, men of letters, and men of affairs.

20. On the creative side are men who spend their time in laboratories, or over microscopes and telescopes, side by side with the men who dominate the commercial, political, and scientific world; on the negative side or men who spend their time investigating law and precedent, men who mistake theology for religion, statesmen who mistake might for right, and all the millions who seem to prefer precedent to progress, who are eternally looking backward instead of forward, who see only the world without, but know nothing of the world within.

21. In the last analysis there are but these two classes. All men will have to take their place on one side or the other; they will have to go forward, or go back. There is no standing still in a world where all is motion; it is this attempt to stand still that gives sanction and force to arbitrary and unequal codes of law.

22. That we are in a period of transition is evidenced by the unrest which is everywhere apparent. The complaint of humanity is as a roll of heaven's artillery, commencing with low and threatening notes and increasing until the sound is sent from cloud to cloud, and the lightning splits the air and earth.

23. The sentries who patrol the most advanced outposts of the Industrial, Political, and Religious world are calling anxiously to each other. What of the night? The danger and insecurity of the position they occupy and attempt to hold is becoming more apparent every hour. The dawn of a new era necessarily declares that the existing order of things cannot much longer be.

24. The issue between the old regime and the new, the crux of the social problem, is entirely a question of conviction in the minds of the people as to the nature of the Universe. When they realize that the transcendent force of spirit or mind of the Cosmos is within each individual, it will be possible to frame laws that shall consider the liberties and rights of the many instead of the privileges of the few.

25. As long as the people regard the Cosmic power as a power non-human and alien to humanity, so long will it be comparatively easy for a supposed privileged class to rule by Divine right in spite of every protest of social sentiment. The real interest of democracy is therefore to exalt, emancipate and recognize the divinity of the human spirit; to recognize that all power is from within. That no human being has any more power than any other human being, except such as may willingly be delegated to him. The old regime would have us believe that the law was superior to the lawmakers; herein is the gist of the social crime of every form of privilege and personal inequality, the institutionalizing of the fatalistic doctrine of Divine election.

26. The Divine Mind is the Universal Mind. It makes no exceptions, it plays no favorites; it does not act through sheer caprice or from anger, jealousy or wrath; neither can it be flattered, cajoled or moved by sympathy or petition to supply man with some need which he thinks necessary for his happiness or even his existence. The Divine Mind makes no exceptions in favor any individual, but when the individual understands and realizes his Unity with the Universal principle he will appear to be favored because he will have found the source of all health, all wealth, and all power.

27. For your exercise this week, concentrate on the Truth. Try to realize that the Truth shall make you free; that is, nothing can permanently stand in the way of your perfect success when you learn to apply the scientifically correct thought methods and principles. Realize that you are externalizing in your environment your inherent soul potencies. Realize that the Silence offers an ever available and almost unlimited opportunity for awakening the highest conception of Truth. Try to comprehend that Omnipotence itself is absolute silence; all else is change, activity, limitation. Silent thought concentration is therefore the true method of reaching, awakening, and then expressing the wonderful potential power of the world within.

"The possibilities of thought training are infinite, its consequence eternal, and yet few take the pains to direct their thinking into channels that will do them good, but instead leave all to chance." - Marden

PART TWENTY-ONE Study Questions with Answers

201. What is the real secret of power? The consciousness of power, because whatever we become conscious of is invariably manifested in the objective world, is brought forth into tangible expression.

202. What is the source of this power? The Universal Mind from which all things proceed, and which is one and indivisible.

203. How is this power being manifested? Through the individual; each individual is a channel whereby this energy is being differentiated in form.

204. How may we connect with this Omnipotence? Our ability to think is our ability to act on this Universal Energy, and what we think is what is produced or created in the objective world.

205. What is the result of this discovery? The result is nothing less than marvelous; it opens unprecedented and limitless opportunity.

206. How, then, may we eliminate imperfect conditions? By becoming conscious of our Unity with the source of all power.

207. What is one of the distinctive characteristics of the Master Mind? He thinks big thoughts, he holds ideas large enough to counteract and destroy all petty and annoying obstacles.

208. How do experiences come to us? Through the law of attraction.

209. How is this law brought into operation? By our predominant mental attitude.

210. What is the issue between the old regime and the new? A question of conviction as to the nature of the Universe. The old regime is trying to cling to the fatalistic doctrine of Divine election. The new regime recognizes the divinity of the individual, the democracy of humanity.

INTRODUCTION - PART TWENTY-TWO

In Part Twenty-two you will find that thoughts are spiritual seeds, which, when planted in the subconscious mind, have a tendency to sprout and grow, but unfortunately the fruit is frequently not to our liking.

The various forms of inflammation, paralysis, nervousness and diseased conditions generally, are the manifestation of fear, worry, care, anxiety, jealousy, hatred and similar thought.

The life processes are carried on by two distinct methods: first, the taking up and making use of nutritive material necessary for constructing cells; second, breaking down and excreting the waste material.

All life is based upon these constructive and destructive activities, and as food, water and air are the only requisites necessary for the construction of cells, it would seem that the problem of prolonging life indefinitely would not be a very difficult one.

However strange it may seem, it is the second or destructive activity that is, with rare exception, the cause of all disease. The waste material accumulates and saturates the tissues, which causes autointoxication. This may be partial or general. In the first case the disturbance will be local; in the second place it will affect the whole system.

The problem then before us in the healing of disease is to increase the inflow and distribution of vital energy throughout the system, and this can only be done by eliminating thoughts of fear, worry, care, anxiety, jealousy, hatred, and every other destructive thought, which tend to tear down and destroy the nerves and glands which control the excretion and elimination of poisonous and waste matter.

"Nourishing foods and strengthening tonics" cannot bestow life, because these are but secondary manifestations to life. The primary manifestation of life and how you may get in touch with it is explained in the Part which I have the privilege of enclosing herewith.

PART TWENTY-TWO

1. Knowledge is of priceless value, because by applying knowledge we can make our future what we wish it to be. When we realize that our present character, our present environment, our present ability, our present physical condition are all the result of past methods of thinking, we shall begin to have some conception of the value of knowledge.

2. If the state of our health is not all that could be desired, let us examine our method of thinking; let us remember that every thought produces an impression on the mind. Every impression is a seed which will sink into the subconscious and form a tendency; the tendency will be to attract other similar thoughts and before we know it we shall have a crop which must be harvested.

3. If these thoughts contain disease germs, the harvest will be sickness, decay, weakness, and failure. The question is, what are we thinking, what are we creating, what is the harvest to be?

4. If there is any physical condition which it is necessary to change, the law governing visualization will be found effective. Make a mental image of physical perfection, hold it in the mind until it is absorbed by the consciousness. Many have eliminated chronic ailments in a few weeks by this method, and thousands have overcome and destroyed all manner of ordinary physical disturbances by this method in a few days, sometimes in a few minutes.

5. It is through the law of vibration that the mind exercises this control over the body. We know that every mental action is a vibration, and we know that all form is simply a mode of motion, a rate of vibration. Therefore, any given vibration immediately modifies every atom in the body, every life cell is affected and an entire chemical change is made in every group of life cells.

6. Everything in the Universe is what it is by virtue of its rate of vibration. Change the rate of vibration and you change the nature, quality and form. The vast panorama of nature, both visible and invisible, is being constantly changed by simply changing the rate of vibration, and as thought is a vibration we can also exercise this power. We can change the vibration and thus produce any condition which we desire to manifest in our bodies.

7. We are all using this power every minute. The trouble is most of us are using it unconsciously and thus producing undesirable results. The problem is to use it intelligently and produce only desirable results. This should not be difficult, because we all have had sufficient experience to know what produces pleasant vibration in the body, and we also know the causes which produce the unpleasant and disagreeable sensations.

8. All that is necessary is to consult our own experience. When our thought has been uplifted, progressive, constructive, courageous, noble, kind or in any other way desirable, we have set in motion vibrations which brought about certain results. When our thought has been filled with envy, hatred, jealousy, criticism or any of the other thousand and one forms of discord, certain vibrations were set in motion which brought about certain other results of a different nature, and each of these rates of vibration, if kept up, crystallized in form. In the first case the result was mental, moral and physical health, and in the second case, discord, inharmony and disease.

9. We can understand, then, something of the power which the mind possesses over the body.

10. The objective mind has certain effects on the body which are readily recognized. Someone says something to you which strikes you as ludicrous and you laugh, possibly until your whole body shakes, which shows that thought has control over the muscles of your body; or someone says something which excites your sympathy and your eyes fill with tears, which shows that thought controls the glands of your body; or someone says something which makes you angry and the blood mounts to your cheek, which shows that thought controls the circulation of your blood. But as these experiences are all the results of the action of your objective mind over the body, the results are of a temporary nature; they soon pass away and leave the situation as it was before.

11. Let us see how the action of the subconscious mind over the body differs. You receive a wound; thousands of cells being the work of healing at once. In a few days or a few weeks the work is complete. You may even break a bone. No surgeon on earth can weld the parts together (I am not referring to the insertion of rods or other devices to strengthen or replace bones). He may set the bone for you, and the subjective mind will immediately begin the process of welding the parts together, and in a short time the bone is as solid as it ever was. You may swallow poison; the subjective mind will immediately discover the danger and make violent efforts to eliminate it. You may become infected with a dangerous germ; the subjective will at once commence to build a wall around the infected area and destroy the infection by absorbing it in the white blood corpuscles which it supplies for the purpose.

12. These processes of the subconscious mind usually proceed without our personal knowledge or direction, and so long as we do not interfere the result is perfect, but, as these millions of repair cells are all intelligent and respond to our thought, they are often paralyzed and rendered impotent by our thoughts of fear, doubt, and anxiety. They are like an army of workmen, ready to start an important piece of work, but every time they get started on the undertaking a strike is called, or plans changed, until they finally get discouraged and give up.

13. The way to health is founded on the law of vibration, which is the basis of all science, and this law is brought into operation by the mind, the "world within." It is a matter of individual effort and practice. Our world of power is within; if we are wise we shall not waste time and effort in trying to deal with effects as we find them in the "world without," which is only an external, a reflection.

14. We shall always find the cause in the "world within"; by changing the cause, we change the effect.

15. Every cell in your body is intelligent and will respond to your direction. The cells are all creators and will create the exact pattern which you give them.

16. Therefore, when perfect images are placed before the subjective, the creative energies will build a perfect body.

17. Brain cells are constructed in the same way. The quality of the brain is governed by the state of mind, or mental attitude, so that if undesirable mental attitudes are conveyed to the subjective they will in turn be transferred to the body; we can therefore readily see that if we wish the body to manifest health, strength and vitality this must be the predominant thought.

18. We know then that every element of the human body is the result of a rate of vibration.

19. We know that mental action is a rate of vibration.

20. We know that a higher rate of vibration governs, modifies, controls, changes, or destroys a lower rate of vibration.

21. We know that the rate of vibration is governed by the character of brain cells, and finally,

22. We know how to create these brain cells; therefore,

23. We know how to make any physical change in the body we desire, and having secured a working knowledge of the power of mind to this extent, we have come to know that there is practically no limitation which can be placed upon our ability to place ourselves in harmony with natural law, which is omnipotent.

24. This influence or control over the body by mind is coming to be more and more generally understood, and many physicians are now giving the matter their earnest attention. Dr. Albert T. Shofield, who has written several important books on the subject, says, "The subject of mental therapeutics is still ignored in medical works generally. In our physiologies no references is made to the central controlling power that rules the body for its good, and the power of the mind over the body is seldom spoken of".

25. No doubt many physicians treat nervous diseases of functional origin wisely and well, but what we contend is that the knowledge they display was taught at no school, was learned from no book, but it is intuitive and empirical.

26. This is not as it should be. The power of mental therapeutics should be the subject of careful, special and scientific teaching in every medical school. We might pursue the subject of maltreatment, or want of treatment, further in detail and describe the disastrous results of neglected cases; but the task is an invidious one.

27. There can be no doubt that few patients are aware how much they can do for themselves. What the patient can do for himself, the forces he can set in motion are as yet unknown. We are inclined to believe that they are far greater than most imagine, and will undoubtedly be used more and more. Mental therapeutics may be directed by the patient himself to calming the mind in excitement, by arousing feelings of joy, hope, faith, and love; by suggesting motives for exertion, by regular mental work, by diverting the thoughts from the malady.

28. For your exercise this week, concentrate on Tennyson's beautiful lines "Speak to Him, thou, for He hears, and spirit with spirit can meet, Closer is He than breathing, and nearer than hands and feet." Then try to realize that when you do "Speak to Him" you are in touch with Omnipotence.

29. This realization and recognition of this Omnipresent power will quickly destroy any and every form of sickness or suffering and substitute harmony and perfection. Then remember there are those who seem to think that sickness and suffering are sent by God; if so, every physician, every surgeon and every Red Cross nurse is defying the will of God and hospitals and sanitariums are places of rebellion instead of houses of mercy. Of course, this quickly reasons itself into an absurdity, but there are many who still cherish the idea.

30. Then let the thought rest on the fact that until recently, theology has been trying to teach an impossible Creator, one who created beings capable of sinning and then allowed them to be eternally punished for such sins. Of course the necessary outcome of such extraordinary ignorance was to create fear instead of love, and so, after two thousand years of this kind of propaganda, Theology is now busily engaged in apologizing for Christendom.

31. You will then more readily appreciate the ideal man, the man made in the image and likeness of God, and you will more readily appreciate the all-originating Mind that forms, upholds, sustains, originates, and creates all there is. "All are but parts of one stupendous whole, whose body nature is, and God the soul." Opportunity follows perception; action follows inspiration; growth follows knowledge; eminence flows progress. Always the spiritual first, then the transformation into the infinite and illimitable possibilities of achievement.

PART TWENTY-TWO Study Questions with Answers

211. How may sickness be eliminated? By placing ourselves in harmony with Natural Law which is Omnipotent.

212. What is the process? A realization that man is a spiritual being and that this spirit must necessarily be perfect.

213. What is the result? A conscious recognition of this perfection - first intellectually, then emotionally - brings about a manifestation of this perfection.

214. Why is this so? Because thought is spiritual and therefore creative and correlates with its object and brings it into manifestation.

215. What Natural Law is brought into operation? The Law of Vibration.

216. Why does this govern? Because a higher rate of vibration governs, modifies, controls, changes, or destroys a lower rate of vibration.

217. Is this system of mental therapeutics generally recognized? Yes, there are literally millions of people in this country who make use of it in one form or another (and obviously many more world-wide).

218. What is the result of this system of thought? For the first time in the world's history, every man's highest reasoning faculty can be satisfied by a demonstrable truth which is now fast flooding the world.

219. Is this system applicable to other forms of supply? It will meet every human requirement or necessity.

220. Is this system scientific or religious? Both. True science and true religion are twin sisters; where one goes, the other necessarily follows.

INTRODUCTION - PART TWENTY-THREE

In the part which I have the honor to transmit here with you, you will find that money weaves itself into the entire fabric of our very existence; that the law of success is service; that we get what we give, and for this reason we should consider it a great privilege to be able to give.

We have found that thought is the creative activity behind every constructive enterprise. We can therefore give nothing of more practical value than our thought.

Creative thought requires attention, and the power of attention is, as we have found, the weapon of the Super-man. Attention develops concentration, and concentration develops Spiritual Power, and Spiritual Power is the mightiest force in existence.

This is the science which embraces all sciences. It is the art which, above all arts, is relevant to human life. In the mastery of this science and this art there is opportunity for unending progression. Perfection in this is not acquired in six days, nor in six weeks, nor in six months. It is the labor of life. Not to go forward is to go backward.

It is inevitable that the entertainment of positive, constructive and unselfish thoughts should have a far-reaching effect for good. Compensation is the keynote of the universe. Nature is constantly seeking to strike an equilibrium. Where something is sent out something must be received, else there should be a vacuum formed. By observance of this rule you cannot fail to profit in such measure as to amply justify your effort along this line.

PART TWENTY-THREE

1. The money consciousness is an attitude of mind; it is the open door to the arteries of commerce. It is the receptive attitude. Desire is the attractive force which sets the current in motion and fear is the great obstacle by which the current is stopped or completely reversed, turned away from us.

2. Fear is just the opposite from money consciousness. It is poverty consciousness, and as the law is unchangeable we get exactly what we give. If we fear, we get what we feared. Money weaves itself into the entire fabric of our very existence; it engages the best thought of the best minds.

3. We make money by making friends, and we enlarge our circle of friends by making money for them, by helping them, by being of service to them. The first law of success then is service, and this in turn is built on integrity and justice. The man who at least is not fair in his intention is simply ignorant; he has missed the fundamental law of all exchange; he is impossible; he will lose surely and certainly; he may not know it, he may think he is winning, but he is doomed to certain defeat. He cannot cheat the Infinite. The law of compensation will demand of him an eye for an eye and a tooth for a tooth.

4. The forces of life are volatile. They are composed of our thoughts and ideals and these in turn are molded into form. Our problem is to keep an open mind, to constantly reach out for the new, to recognize opportunity, to be interested in the race rather than the goal, for the pleasure is in the pursuit rather than the possession.

5. You can make a money magnet of yourself, but to do so you must first consider how you can make money for other people. If you have the necessary insight to perceive and utilize opportunities and favorable conditions and recognize values, you can put yourself in position to take advantage of them, but your greatest success will come as you are enabled to assist others. What benefits one must benefit all.

6. A generous thought is filled with strength and vitality. A selfish thought contains the germs of dissolution; it will disintegrate and pass away. Great financiers are simply channels for the distribution of wealth. Enormous amounts come and go, but it would be as dangerous to stop the outgo as the income. Both ends must remain open, and so our greatest success will come as we recognize that it is just as essential to give as to get.

7. If we recognize the Omnipotent power that is the source of all supply, we will adjust our consciousness to this supply in such a way that it will constantly attract all that is necessary to itself and we shall find that the more we give the more we get. Giving in this sense implies service. The banker gives his money, the merchant gives his goods, the author gives his thought, the workman gives his skill; all have something to give, but the more they can give, the more they get, and the more they get the more they are enabled to give.

8. The financier gets much because he gives much. He thinks -- he is seldom a man that lets anyone else do his thinking for him. He wants to know how results are to be secured. You must show him; when you can do this he will furnish the means by which hundreds or thousands may profit, and in proportion as they are successful will he be successful. Morgan, Rockefeller, Carnegie and others did not get rich because they lost money for other people; on the contrary, it is because they made money for other people that they became the wealthiest men in the wealthiest country on the globe.

9. The average person is entirely innocent of any deep thinking. He accepts the ideas of others and repeats them, in very much the same way as a parrot. This is readily seen when we understand the method which is used to form public opinion, and this docile attitude on the part of a large majority who seem perfectly willing to let a few persons do all their thinking for them is what enables a few men in a great many countries to usurp all the avenues of power and hold the millions in subjection. Creative thinking requires attention.

10. The power of attention is called concentration. This power is directed by the will. For this reason, we must refuse to concentrate or think of anything except the things we desire. Many are constantly concentrating upon sorrow, loss and discord of every kind; as thought is creative it necessarily follows that this concentration inevitably leads to more loss, more sorrow and more discord. How could it be otherwise? On the other hand, when we meet with success, gain, or any other desirable condition, we naturally concentrate upon the effects of these things and thereby create more, and so it follows that much leads to more.

11. How an understanding of this principle can be utilized in the business world is well told by an associate of mine:

12. "Spirit, whatever else it may or may not be, must be considered as the Essence of Consciousness, the Substance of Mind, the reality underlying Thought. And as all ideas are phases of the activity of Consciousness, Mind or Thought, it follows that in Spirit, and in it alone, is to be found the Ultimate Fact, the Real Thing, or Idea."

13. This being admitted, does it not seem reasonable to hold that a true understanding of Spirit and its laws of manifestation would be about the most "practical" thing that a "practical" person can hope to find? Does it not seem certain that if the "practical" men of the world could but realize this fact, they would "fall all over themselves" in getting to the place in which they might obtain such knowledge of spiritual things and laws? These men are not fools; they need only to grasp this fundamental fact in order to move in the direction of that which is the essence of all achievement.

14. Let me give you a concrete example. I know a man in Chicago whom I had always

15. considered to be quite materialistic. He had made several successes in life, and also several failures. The last time I had a talk with him he was practically "down and out," as compared with his former business condition. It looked as if he had indeed reached "the end of his rope," for he was well advanced into the stage of middle age, and new ideas came more slowly and less frequently to him than in former years.

16. He said to me, in substance: "I know that all things that 'work out' in business are the result of Thought; any fool knows that. Just now, I seem to be short on thoughts and good ideas. But, if this 'All-Mind' teaching is correct, it should be possible for the individual to attain a 'direct connection' with Infinite Mind; and in Infinite Mind there must be the possibility of all kinds of good ideas which a man of my courage and experience could put to practical use in the business world, and make a big success thereof. It looks good to me, and I am going to look into it."

17. This was several years ago. The other day I heard of this man again. Talking to a friend, I said: "What has come of our old friend X? Has he ever gotten on his feet again?" The friend looked at me in amazement. "Why," said he, "don't you know about X's great success? He is the Big Man in the '_____ Company' (naming a concern which has made a phenomenal success during the last eighteen months and is now well-known, by reason of its advertisements, from one end of the country to another, and also abroad). He is the man who supplied the BIG IDEA for that concern. Why, he is about a half-million to the good and is moving rapidly toward the million mark, all in the space of eighteen months." I had not connected this man with the enterprise mentioned, although I knew of the wonderful success of the company in question. Investigation has shown that the story is true, and that the above stated facts are not exaggerated in the slightest.

18. Now, what do you think of that? To me, it means that this man actually made the "direct connection" with Infinite Mind -- Spirit -- and, having found it, he set it to work for him. He "used it in his business."

19. Does this sound sacrilegious or blasphemous? I hope not; I do not mean it to be so. Take away the implication of Personality, or Magnified Human Nature, from the conception of the "The Infinite," and you have left the conception of an Infinite Presence-Power, the Quintessence of which is Consciousness -- in fact, at the last, Spirit. As this man also, at the last, must be considered as a manifestation of Spirit, there is nothing sacrilegious in the idea that he, being Spirit, should so harmonize himself with his Origin and Source that he would be able to manifest at least a minor degree of its Power. All of us do this, more or less, when we use our minds in the direction of Creative Thought. This man did more; he went about it in an intensely "practical" manner.

20. I have not consulted him about his method of procedure, though I intend doing so at the first opportunity, but he not only drew upon the Infinite Supply for the ideas which he needed (and which formed the seed of his success), but that he also used the Creative Power of Thought in building up for himself an Idealistic Pattern of that which he hoped to manifest in material form; adding thereto, changing, improving its detail, from time to time -- proceeding from the general outline to the finished detail. I judge this to be the facts of the case, not alone from my recollection of the conversation a few years ago, but also because I have found the same thing to be true in the cases of other prominent men who have made similar manifestation of Creative Thought.

21. Those who may shrink from this idea of employing the Infinite Power to aid one in his work in the material world should remember that if the Infinite objected in the least to such a procedure the thing could never happen. The Infinite is quite able to take care of Itself.

22. "Spirituality" is quite "practical," very "practical," intensely "practical." It teaches that Spirit is the Real Thing, the Whole Thing, and that Matter is but plastic stuff which Spirit is able to create, mould, manipulate, and fashion to its will. Spirituality is the most "practical" thing in the world -- the only really and absolutely "practical" thing that there is!

23. This week, concentrate on the fact that man is not a body with a spirit, but a spirit with a body, and that it is for this reason that his desires are incapable of any permanent satisfaction in anything not spiritual. Money is therefore of no value except to bring about the conditions which we desire, and these conditions are necessarily harmonious. Harmonious conditions necessitate sufficient supply, so that if there appears to be any lack, we should realize that the idea or soul of money is service, and as this thought takes form, channels of supply will be opened, and you will have the satisfaction of knowing that spiritual methods are entirely practical.

"We have discovered that premeditated, orderly thinking for a purpose matures that purpose into fixed form, so that we may be absolutely sure of the result of our dynamic experiment."

-Francis Larimer Warner

PART TWENTY-THREE Study Questions

221. What is the first law of success? Service.

222. How may we be of the most service? Have an open mind; be interested in the race rather than the goal, in the pursuit rather than possession.

223. What is the result of a selfish thought? It contains the germs of dissolution.

224. How will our greatest success be achieved? By a recognition of the fact that it is just as essential to give as to receive.

225. Why do financiers frequently meet with great success? Because they do their own thinking.

226. Why do the great majority in every country remain the docile and apparently willing tools of the few? Because they let the few do all their thinking for them.

227. What is the effect of concentrating upon sorrow and loss? More sorrow and more loss.

228. What is the effect of concentrating upon gain? More gain.

229. Is this principle used in the business world? It is the only principle which is ever used, or ever can be used; there is no other principle. The fact that it may be used unconsciously does not alter the situation.

230. What is the practical application of this principle? The fact that success is an effect, not a cause, and if we wish to secure the effect we must ascertain the cause, or idea or thought by which the effect is created.

"Nurture your mind with great thoughts; to believe in the heroic makes heroes." - Disraeli

INTRODUCTION - PART TWENTY-FOUR

Enclosed you will find Part Twenty-four, your final lesson of this course.

If you have practiced each of the exercises a few minutes every day as suggested, you will have found that you can get out of life exactly what you wish by first putting into life that which you wish, and you will probably agree with the student who said: "The thought is almost overwhelming, so vast, so available, so definite, so reasonable and so usable."

The fruit of this knowledge is, as it were, a gift of the Gods. It is the "truth" that makes men free, not only free from every lack and limitation, but free from sorrow, worry and care, and is it not wonderful to realize that this law is no respecter of persons, that it makes no difference what your habit of thought may be? The way has been prepared.

If you are inclined to be religious, the greatest religious teacher the world has ever known made the way so plain that all may follow. If your mental bias is toward physical science, the law will operate with mathematical certainty. If you are inclined to be philosophical, Plato or Emerson may be your teacher, but in either case you may reach degrees of power to which it is impossible to assign any limit.

An understanding of this principle, I believe, is the secret for which the ancient Alchemists vainly sought, because it explains how gold in the mind may be transmuted into gold in the heart and in the hand.

PART TWENTY-FOUR

1. When the scientists first put the Sun in the center of the Solar System and sent the earth spinning around it, there was immense surprise and consternation. The whole idea was self-evidently false; nothing was more certain than the movement of the Sun across the sky, and anyone could see it descend behind the western hills and sink into the sea. Scholars raged and scientists rejected the idea as absurd, yet the evidence has finally carried conviction in the minds of all.

2. We speak of a bell as a "sounding body," yet we know that all the bell can do is to produce vibrations in the air. When these vibrations come at the rate of sixteen per second, they cause a sound to be heard in the mind. It is also possible for the mind to hear vibrations up to the rate of 38,000 vibrations per second. When the number increases beyond this, all is silence again, so that we know that the sound is not in the bell, it is in our own mind.

3. We speak and even think of the Sun as "giving light." Yet we know it is simply giving forth energy which produces vibrations in the ether at the rate of four hundred trillion a second, causing what are termed light waves, so that we know that we call light is simply a form of energy, and that the only light there is, is the sensation caused in the mind by the motion of the waves. When the number increases, the light changes in color, each change in color being caused by shorter and more rapid vibrations; so that although we speak of the rose as being red, the grass as being green, or the sky as being blue, we know that the colors exist only in our minds, and are the sensations experienced by us as the result of the vibrations of light waves. When the vibrations are reduced below four hundred trillion a second, they no longer affect us as light, but we experience the sensation of heat. It is evident, therefore, that we cannot depend upon the evidence of the senses for our information concerning the realities of things; if we did we should believe that the sun moved, that the world was flat instead of round, that the stars were bits of light instead of vast suns.

4. The whole range then of the theory and practice of any system of metaphysics consists in knowing the Truth concerning yourself and the world in which you live; in knowing that in order to express harmony, you must think harmony, in order to express health you must think health, and in order to express abundance you must think abundance. To do this you must reverse the evidence of the senses.

5. When you come to know that every form of disease, sickness, lack and limitation are simply the result of wrong thinking, you will have come to know "the Truth which shall make you free." You will see how mountains may be removed. If these mountains consist only of doubt, fear, distrust or other forms of discouragement, they are nonetheless real, and they need not only to be removed, but to be "cast into the sea."

6. Your real work consists in convincing yourself of the truth of these statements. When you have succeeded in doing this you will have no difficulty in thinking the truth, and as has been shown, the truth contains a vital principle and will manifest itself.

7. Those who heal diseases by mental methods have come to know this truth; they demonstrate it in their lives and the lives of others daily. They know that life, health and abundance are Omnipresent, filling all space, and they know that those who allow disease or lack of any kind to manifest have as yet not come into an understanding of this great law.

8. As all conditions are thought creations and therefore entirely mental, disease and lack are simply mental conditions in which the person fails to perceive the truth; as soon as the error is removed, the condition is removed.

9. The method for removing this error is to go into the Silence and know the Truth. As all mind is one mind, you can do this for yourself or anyone else. If you have learned to form mental images of the conditions desired, this will be the easiest and quickest way to secure results; if not, results can be accomplished by argument, by the process of convincing yourself absolutely of the truth of your statement.

10. Remember, and this is one of the most difficult as well as most wonderful statements to grasp: Remember that no matter what the difficulty is, no matter where it is, no matter who is affected, you have no patient but yourself; you have nothing to do but to convince yourself of the truth which you desire to see manifested.

11. This is an exact scientific statement in accordance with every system of Metaphysics in existence, and no permanent results are ever secured in any other way.

12. Every form of concentration, forming Mental Images, Argument, and Auto-Suggestion are all simply methods by which you are enabled to realize the Truth.

13. If you desire to help someone, to destroy some form of lack, limitation or error, the correct method is not to think of the person whom you wish to help; the intention to help them is entirely sufficient, as this puts you in mental touch with the person. Then drive out of your own mind any belief of lack, limitation, disease, danger, difficulty or whatever the trouble might be. As soon as you have succeeded is doing this the result will have been accomplished, and the person will be free.

14. But remember that thought is creative and consequently every time you allow your thought to rest on any inharmonious condition, you must realize that such conditions are apparent only, they have no reality; that spirit is the only reality and it can never be less than perfect.

15. All thought is a form of energy, a rate of vibration, but a thought of the Truth is the highest rate of vibration known and consequently destroys every form of error in exactly the same way that light destroys darkness. No form of error can exist when the "Truth" appears, so that your entire mental work consists in coming into an understanding of the Truth. This will enable you to overcome every form of lack, limitation or disease of any kind.

16. We can get no understanding of the truth from the world without. The world without is relative only. Truth is absolute. We must therefore find it in the "world within."

17. To train the mind to see Truth only is to express true conditions only. Our ability to do this will be an indication as to the progress we are making.

18. The absolute truth is that the "I" is perfect and complete. The real "I" is spiritual and can therefore never be less than perfect; it can never have any lack, limitation, or disease. The flash of genius does not have origin in the molecular motion of the brain. It is inspired by the ego, the spiritual "I" which is one with the Universal Mind, and it is our ability to recognize this Unity which is the cause of all inspiration, all genius. These results are far-reaching and have effect upon generations yet to come. They are the pillars of fire which mark the path that millions follow.

19. Truth is not the result of logical training or of experimentation, or even of observation; it is the product of a developed consciousness. Truth within a Caesar manifests in a Caesar's deportment, in his life and his action, his influence upon social forms and progress. Your life and your actions and your influence in the world will depend upon the degree of truth which you are enabled to perceive, for truth will not manifest in creeds but in conduct.

20. Truth manifests in character, and the character of a man should be the interpretation of his religion, or what to him is truth, and this will in turn be evidenced in the character of his possessions. If a man complains of the drift of his fortune, he is just as unjust to himself as if he should deny rational truth, though it stands patent and irrefutable.

21. Our environment and the innumerable circumstances and accidents of our lives already exist in the subconscious personality which attracts to itself the mental and physical material which is congenial to its nature. Thus, our future is being determined from our present, and if there should be apparent injustice in any feature or phase of our personal life, we must look within for the cause, try to discover the mental fact which is responsible for the outward manifestation.

22. It is this truth which makes you "free", and it is the conscious knowledge of this truth which will enable you to overcome every difficulty.

23. The conditions with which you meet in the world without are invariably the result of the conditions obtaining in the world within, therefore it follows with scientific accuracy that by holding the perfect ideal in mind you can bring about ideal conditions in your environment.

24. If you see only the incomplete - the imperfect, the relative, the limited, these conditions will manifest in your life; but if you train your mind to see and realize the spiritual ego - the "I" which is forever perfect and complete, harmonious, wholesome, and healthful conditions only will be manifested.

25. As thought is creative, and the truth is the highest and most perfect thought which anyone can think, it is self-evident that to think the truth is to create that which is true, and it is again evident that when truth comes into being that which is false must cease to be.

26. The Universal Mind is the totality of all mind which is in existence. Spirit is Mind, because spirit is intelligent. The words are, therefore, synonymous.

27. The difficulty with which you have to contend is to realize that mind is not individual. It is omnipresent. It exists everywhere. In other words, there is no place where it is not. It is, therefore, Universal.

28. Men have, heretofore, generally used the word "God" to indicate this Universal creative principle; but the word "God" does not convey the right meaning. Most people understand this word to mean something outside of themselves, while exactly the contrary is the fact. It is our very life. Without it we would be dead. We would cease to exist. The minute the spirit leaves the body, we are as nothing. Therefore, spirit is really all there is of us.

29. Now the only activity which the spirit possesses is the power to think. Therefore, thought must be creative, because spirit is creative. This creative power is impersonal, and your ability to think is your ability to control it and make use of it for the benefit of yourself and others.

30. When the truth of this statement is realized, understood, and appreciated, you will have come into possession of the Master-Key; but remember that only those who are wise enough to understand, broad enough to weigh the evidence, firm enough to follow their own judgment, and strong enough to make the sacrifice exacted, may enter and partake.

31. This week, try to realize that this is truly a wonderful world in which we live, that you are a wonderful being, that many are awakening to a knowledge of the Truth, and as fast as they awake and come into a knowledge of the "things which have been prepared for them", they, too realize that "Eye hath not seen, nor ear heard, neither hath it entered into the heart of man" the splendors which exist for those who find themselves in the Promised Land. They have crossed the river of judgment and have arrived at the point of discrimination between the true and the false, and have found that all they ever willed or dreamed was but a faint concept of the dazzling reality.

"Though an inheritance of acres may be bequeathed, an inheritance of knowledge and wisdom cannot. The wealthy man may pay others for doing his work for him, but it is impossible to get his thinking done for him by another or to purchase any kind of self-culture."

- S. Smiles

PART TWENTY-FOUR Study Questions with Answers

231. Upon what principle does the theory and practice of every system of Metaphysics in existence depend? Upon a knowledge of the "Truth" concerning yourself and the world in which you live.

232. What is the "Truth" concerning yourself? The real "I" or ego is spiritual and can therefore never be less than perfect.

233. What is the method of destroying any form of error? To absolutely convince yourself of the "Truth" concerning the condition which you wish to see manifested.

234. Can we do this for others? The Universal Mind in which "we live and move and have our being" is one and indivisible; it is therefore just as possible to help others as to help ourselves.

235. What is the Universal Mind? The totality of all mind in existence.

236. Where is the Universal Mind? The Universal Mind is omnipresent; it exists everywhere. There is no place where it is not. It is therefore within us. It is "The World within". It is our spirit, our life.

237. What is the nature of the Universal Mind? It is spiritual and consequently creative. It seeks to express itself in form.

238. How may we act on the Universal Mind? Our ability to think is our ability to act on the Universal Mind and bring it into manifestation for the benefit of ourselves or others.

239. What is meant by thinking? Clear, decisive, calm, deliberate, sustained thought with a definite end in view.

240. What will be the result? You will also be able to say, "It is not I that doeth the works, but the 'Father' that dwelleth within me, He doeth the works." You will come to know that the "Father" is the Universal Mind and that He does really and truly dwell within you. In other words, you will come to know that the wonderful promises made in the Bible are fact, not fiction, and can be demonstrated by anyone having sufficient understanding.

"Temples have their sacred images, and we see what influence they have always had over a great part of mankind; but, in truth, the ideas and images in men's minds are the invisible powers that constantly govern them; and to these they all pay universally a ready submission." - Jonathan Edwards

CPSIA information can be obtained at www.ICGtesting.com
Printed in the USA
LVOW11s2157140713

342854LV00005B/88/A